Racing in the Street

Early Cafe Racer Years

Billy Wells

Also by this author:

Snapshots of the Hippy Trail.

Billy Wells asserts the moral right
to be identified as the author of this book.

Thanks to Ginger Mcrae for most of the pictures and the cover.

Copyright © by Billy Wells 2015

All rights reserved. No part of this book may be reproduced in any form or by any means without permission of the publisher.

RACE AT THE ACE

The first of my few visits to the Ace was in the late summer of 1962 with Paul Cole. I'd met him, one balmy evening, that year, in a race on the Kingston by-pass.
He was two up on a Gold Star and marching on, about 80 or 90, up the Tolworth Rise, in the direction of London.
My mate, Graham Carlton on his Goldie styled Shooting Star and myself on my '60 Bonnie had been to the Tirola; a back alley cafe in Dorking.
Not much happened on the nights I called in there but it was always open and it was near the bottom of Box Hill.
We had blasted round the Mickleham bends, up the rise to Leatherhead, past Chessington Zoo, to pick up the Kingston by-pass at the Ace of Spades. All in the hundreds so by the time we sighted Paul's Goldie, on the A3, we were definitely in the mood for motorcycle sport and, as it turned out, without a doubt, so was he.

Carlt and I took a glance at each other and the old adrenaline level went up a notch.
I kicked down into third and wound it, cheekily, past the Goldie at a hundred and changed up, just to throw down the gauntlet.
I kept it on 110 to the Malden roundabout just so I knew I'd left him in my dust but braking for the roundabout I saw his headlight beam, right next to me, announcing his acceptance of the challenge.
I let the brakes off and dived in fast.
There was space between the cars and he was right behind me, coming out of the roundabout, his headlight beam bobbing and lashing at the road around my bike.
It was going to be a full-on blat.

Winding it up through the gears, scorching past the cars.

The route back to the Caprice, our local cafe, meant turning off at Shannon's Corner but this race was something not to be missed out on.
We stayed on the by-pass, flat out, overtaking everything, round the outside and through every gap available.
Some of the road, back then was single carriageway with bollards; such was the intensity of the competition that it was necessary, occasionally, to go the other side of the keep left signs, against the traffic because the cars had left a lack of space to get through on the right side of the road.
The red mist was down. The Gold Star headlight was chompin at my tail. The race was deferably on.
We caned it all along past the rugby grounds, the Robin Hood gate of Richmond Park, past the KLG tower in Putney Vale and up the rise to Tibbets Corner, where the by-pass ends and London starts. The pace eased; we slowed up and pulled over at the side of the big roundabout for a few words, seeing as the race had been so lively.
Carlt pulled up shortly afterwards with a grin on his face.

That was all right.

Yeah that was great.

That was fast for a Gold Star, two-up.

What you up to now?

We were just going back to the caff in Morden.

We're going up The Bridge for a tea,

Yeah?

Come along.

Alright mate. We all agreed.

A steady, fast ride, through the easy, night time traffic, took us along Wandsworth Road, smartly round the 'S' bends under the railway bridge in Queenstown Road and up to Chelsea Bridge for a cup of tea..
There were a few bikes about, no hangers on, just a few riders stood around chatting and having a tea.
We all got on well and met up, as planned, at noon the next day at the clock tower by Clapham Common tube station. Paul got us to follow him back to his house so he could adjust his chains.
He did it promptly, out in the street, nonchalantly dropped the spanners over his front wall, pulled on his helmet and gloves, started his bike easily and led us through South East London at a lively pace, to the A20, near The Dutch House from where we took a little burn down to Johnsons, a bike cafe just past Brands.

Paul was slow talking and fast riding, he had a DBD 34 Clubmans Gold Star.
A machine spoken of, simply, as a Gold, by the chaps at the Bridge. It had a 5 gallon ally tank in that dark BSA red, complimented by a few wear patches.
We rode a few times with him and his pals but that night at the Ace, when I had, what I guess was, my 15 minutes of fame, there was just Paul, Graham Carlton and me.

We pulled into the Ace and parked up with the other bikes, front wheel in, facing the road.

This is when the Ace was right on the road, before they moved the road.

A little, younger crowd of leather jacketed kids gathered and checked out our bikes as we stood them up on their stands, turned off the petrol and took off our lids.

Usually, when you pulled into one of the big motorbike cafes everyone clocked you but nobody took that much notice.

In amongst the interested parties was somebody a bit lively.

Do you want to sell them pipes?

My Bonnie had a set of high level pipes, one up each side. I'd swapped them with Del, a mate of Paul's. He had a '61 Bonneville; his mate, John, had a '62 Thruxton Bonnie. He'd bought it from Streamline Motorcycles in Dulwich. It had a close box, rearsets, central float, a gallon oil tank and racing number brackets on the rear mudguard stays.

We rode a few times to the coast and to Johnsons.

One time I crashed on the way to Camber Sands. Slid into a country kerb, got flipped off, bending, only, the swinging arm and the Ace bars.

Luckily a brick wall stopped my flight.

John took the bars off my bike, bent them into a usable shape in an iron drain cover and fitted them back on whilst I sat up against the entrance wall of a big old country estate, being plied with a glass of cider and sympathy from kindly local folk.

He was a fast but steady rider, the kind of guy who would let a couple of pounds of air out of his tyres if it started raining.

About a week later John hit a lorry, coming the other way, on the A20 and was killed.

It was in the dip where there was a car scrap yard, down low, to one side with a red and yellow Austin 7 roadster stuck up on a tall pole. Del was right behind him.
He said they were doing about a 100 at the time.

These pipes were rare on the streets of London, only ever seen in film of American desert races, like the Big Bear Run, where the start line was a mile wide and they started the event with a cannon; unleashing a swarm of Triumph, BSA, Norton, Matchless, Royal Enfield, Velocette, Ariel and any kind of scrambler, aiming for the smoke signal on the horizon.
They were great looking pipes.
Del, being unhappy with the power they offered, it being all down the bottom end, had chopped off the ends of the little Trophy style silencers, a bit at a time to get more top end power and ended up with no baffles and the megaphone effect whereby you get hardly any power till about 3500.
Above those revs the power kicks in fiercely, making it quick but very loud.
They were a bit anti social and you had to throttle down and pull the clutch in if you saw a police car but if you kept it on the boil it made the bike very fast.

Have you got a decent set of down pipes?

Yeah.

I'd want 4 quid and your pipes.

I'll give ya free quid.

It's got to be 4.

He shook his head.

Race for the difference. Said a voice in the crowd.

Fuck this. I thought. Stood in the middle of a bunch of leather jacketed nutters, on the tarmac, out front of the hard, bright strip lighting shining through the big iron frame windows of the Ace.

Carlt nudged me in the back.

Go on. He said with his slightly crazed grin on his face.

What bike you got.

A Trophy.

No problem. I thought. I can have him.

OK. I'll race ya.

At that point he bottled out. He didn't want to do it.

I'll ride your bike. Said the guy who suggested the race.

Ok. Said his mate.

The race guy explained how it would be done.

What you do is go out of here, under the bridge, through the lights and some way on there is a gap in the central reservation fence.

You go through the gap and come back down the other carriageway to the lights.
Line up on the green.
Wait until the lights go red.
Then you take off on amber.

He pulled on a battered helmet covered in dents and road rash and disappeared into the crowd to find his mates Trophy.

Paul had experience of this bit of road at speed and mentioned that I should keep between the two manholes under the bridge as there is a raised section in the tarmac either side of them and being on a bit of a curve, hitting that bump at speed could throw a bike sideways, across the road.
I was taking all this in while putting on my helmet and gloves.
I slung my leg over the bike, rocked it off the centre stand, switched on both taps and kicked it into life, giving it a bit of a handful, in that who dares wins approach to the moment.
I didn't turn on the lights because I was going to wring the old bike's neck and I knew it would blow all the bulbs.
I rolled out backwards then put it in first and the crowd opened up to let me through.
At the other end of the car park were some other bikes getting ready for the off.
There was some evil looking stuff there; bikes with exposed chains, like they were straight off the track, bikes with clip-ons down by the bottom yoke, megaphones and push bike lights.
Blokes on mad-arse six-fifties with no helmets or gloves.
Raving, mental, dangerous, urban, highway lunatics if ever you saw them.

We all pulled out onto the road and scorched off towards the bridge with plenty of noise and positioning.
This is around 9 or 10 at night and there is a bit of traffic about.
The pack was pretty close together as we shot through the lights.
I got behind the first two and waited patiently, in line, behind them, on the right hand kerb with the noise of the other bikes lined up behind me.
The traffic charging by on our left.
I made the turn through the gap, between the bits of bushes and bent back wire fence of the central divider and squirted back down the other side of the road, to the lights, giving the bike plenty, to get into the spirit of things.
The lights were green and the first two guys took the two most outside positions, which looked like the safest places to be when you line up on a green light.
I took a spot just off centre, to the left.
When everyone had pulled up there were 6 or 7 of us, most of them I hadn't even seen until now, in fact I'd only been at the Ace for 10 minutes and here I am lined up with a bunch of lunatics, revving the fuck out of their engines, on a green light, on the North Circular, on a Saturday night.
The traffic had pulled up behind us and there was a lot of honking, flashing of headlights and shouting.
I didn't look back but once.
I had the bike in first, giving it some revs.
I figured I'd do racing changes, whereby you only shut the throttle halfway down and only pull the clutch in halfway. It's easier to miss gears but if you get it right it fires you into the next gear at high revs and does give you an advantage over someone doing regular changes.

It, eventually, left a twist in the main shaft keyway like the end of a knife turned in butter but any concern for wear and tear was not being considered at this moment in the proceedings.

On amber everybody launched in an explosion of teenage fury, chrome and screaming engines.
I got flat on the tank right away. Every little helps.
At the end of first gear, with the rev counter needle on the 8, there were three of us in it. At the end of second there was me and another guy up front.
In third I left him behind.
I hung onto third, got between the manhole covers, the bike still jumping all over the place and out from under the bridge.
On the little brick wall outside the Ace, stood loads of bikers, boys and girls, watching to see the outcome of the race. Clocking 105 in third I knocked it into top and sat up to look like I wasn't really trying.
I shot by the café, did a U turn at a set of lights, rode back down the other carriageway and pulled into the car park, rolling into the space next to Paul's Gold and Carlt's Shooting Star, in the row of bikes.
The younger crowd, a couple of years younger or maybe the owners of smaller bikes gathered round as I put my bike on the centre stand and took off my gloves and helmet.
The other riders pulled in and parked up amongst the bikes.

How fast was that?

About a hundred and five.

Have you tuned it?

Done a couple of things, yeah.

I was right pumped up with adrenaline and uneasy with all the attention so I kept my chat down to a suitably moody response worthy of a gunslinger who had just drifted into Tucson and shot it out with Lee Van Cleef, excused myself and joined Paul and Carlt for a tea on the Formica topped table in the very brightly lit caff.
In all the excitement the pipes deal was forgotten.
I didn't fancy swapping over a set of pipes, right then, anyway.

Aaaaaayyyy

CAFÉ SOCIETY

My folks both rode bikes. My Dad had a '38 500 International Norton when they met.
He said that after Dunkirk, where the army had left most of its motorcycles, they'd bought up all the machines from the big bike shops and there was a bike shortage. His station officer in the Fire Service asked him to advertise for bikes for use in the war effort and a few were donated.
He luckily managed to keep hold of the Inter.
One time they were riding from Holborn to Morden when the air raid sirens wailed for the first time in anger.
They said that because it was the first real alert everybody ran for cover. After a while, when it happened daily, things just kept on going as usual until the bombs actually started falling.
This time all the traffic stopped and everyone went into air raid shelters and down into tube stations.
They blasted through the centre of London; Trafalgar Square, Whitehall, its empty streets echoing the sound of the Norton's Brooklands Can, roaring in defiance of the oncoming Nazi menace.
Crossing the river by Westminster Bridge and riding on through the deserted roads of the south, they pulled over and parked outside a shelter at Morden and went in; just to be on the safe side.

He had a '38 Panther with upswept pipes and a sports chair from when I was just a sprog.
My Mum saw a woman riding an outfit one day and took up motorcycling for herself, passing her test on the Panther and buying the first Bantam in 1949 which she rode in a cap, greatcoat, sensible shoes and gauntlets, in her job as a district nurse until 1961 when she bought a new Bantam in red with chrome tank panels.

She did get a mention in the second edition of Classic Bike in Jerry Clayton's article, titled: Memoirs of a By-Pass Cowboy.
She'd put on a bit of a show leaning the bike right over on the curve, outside our local caff, the Caprice because she'd seen my bike amongst the bikes outside.
He laughed and said she'd probably be pretty good round the Mickleham bends.
Steady on. I said. That's my mum.
Jerry had just started hanging out at the Caprice. The other fellahs, just laughed, they had seen her riding about the estate for years.
She rode winter and summer till she was 45 and always liked bikes. The Norton was her favourite.
She used the term Coffee Bar Cowboy to describe poseurs who just hung out in cafes and didn't do any serious riding. I had to tell her I wasn't one of them. I was out there doing it.

You be careful. She'd say. Put your helmet on! You'll end up in the Atkinson Morley! (A hospital in Wimbledon for many a poor soul with damage to his loaf of bread.)
They're nearly all motorcyclists in there!

The Panther took us to race meetings at Brands and to the coast and we always stopped at a cafe on the way there and on the way back. There were an infinite number of roadside cafes to choose from. Every village had at least one and there were loads in the country, some with car parks big enough for lorries and coaches. They were all a bit scruffy. Nobody worried about the décor and when juke boxes arrived people worried even less.
One, I remember, was the Red Arrow on the A29 and the Burmac on the A20, usually just for a cup of tea.
Everyone on the road, in those days, would stop at cafes; there would always be cars and bikes in their car parks.

On a summer's day on some big roads, like the A20, people would stop their bikes and cars, park up and sit on the grassy banks to just watch the traffic which was always worth watching as it was pre-MOT days, not long after the war.
Bald tyres and steaming radiators.
Ancient sidecar outfits with mobs of kids in the chair.
Little, old, pre-war bangers overloaded with grandma and grandchildren smoking and lurching out of town for a day in the country, at a comfortable 20 mph and bikes whizzing down the outside overtaking everything.
Plenty to look at.
We never stopped at those places; we were usually on our way somewhere.

Pulling out of Brands, one day after a race meeting, looking backwards out of the sidecar, I watched a big pack of young fellahs, on their solos, blasting off down Death Hill, back towards London. They looked great, some looking serious in the right gear, some of them without proper jackets and gloves with laughing girlfriends on the back.
A bunch of them disappearing into the distance, some being left behind but all giving it everything in the spirit of the sunny afternoon's entertainment.

Rock and Roll was happening way before it had a name.

Before Rock and Roll music it was all sing-a-longs to a piano in the pub and Knees up Mother Brown. A form of dance I've never grown tired of and an area of the British arts that whilst on my travels to foreign lands I have on occasion introduced to people of other cultures with whom I have had the pleasure to have had a bit of a celebration.

Back then every town had several cafes, big ones, part of a chain, like Joe Lyons or ABC and individual independent, little cafes with style and personalities all their own. Women out at the shops would pop into them for a natter with their friends.
Lunches and breakfasts were served for the working man.
Some stayed open at night and youth would hang about in them.
The juke box was always playing, the grapevine was buzzing, plots were being hatched, jokes were being cracked and romance was in the air.
One or two were modernized with a slight bohemian, bamboo, Expresso Bongo look about the decor.

The Caprice at Morden had a distressed bamboo theme.
There was a big old cactus in the window, which for a while had a spark plug screwed into the top of it along with self tapping screws and small motorcycle parts.
There was another cafe in Morden that stayed open late, Hal's, twinned with Leo's in Mitcham and styled beautifully, years before, as an American ice cream parlour. It was full of a younger up and coming generation of leather jacketed youth, they had the jackets and their first bikes.
There were cafés that were popular on a Sunday morning and night time cafés in other nearby parts of town that would be visited on occasion.
.
The Caprice was small and had bar stools and a narrow bar top to sit by, in front of the window. It was opposite the snooker hall which had a slight underworld vibe to it; like all good snooker halls. The bikes parked along by the snooker hall, in the alley, by the bogs and the police box. The black cabs waited in a rank, outside, to the left of the cafe. The Tube Station and Double Decker Bus Park were across the main drag from there.

There was another side to the place, people would come to sit and have burgers and chips.
A new dining experience in those days.
They would listen to the juke box and soak up the excitement emanating from the motorbike side.

It was a hole in the wall of the Odeon cinema, a magnificent edifice, built in 1932 to cater along with the Gaumont at Rose Hill, for the vast St Helier council estate that was being laid out at the time.
My family moved here from Clerkenwell in 1938. All the families around there came from deeper into London.
It wasn't a cafe like those on major roads where you'd get bikes turning up from all over. It was simply a cafe in a busy side street, a local hangout for youth that were into motorcycles.
It was lively enough at the Caprice and there were different groups of mates within the crowd, some got into racing or the motorcycle business, some just had bikes for a mad 3 or 4 years then went onto cars but would still call in at the cafe to hear and tell more stories.
There were bike cafes in every part of London, as elsewhere, where bunches of mates would meet and there was usually someone who knew someone from a neighbouring hang out. We were all teenagers and generally glad to meet other young souls that were into bikes. Any rivalries sorted out scorching through the streets or down the by-passes.
The Caprice flourished, probably because it was a focal point within easy striking distance of the Sutton by-pass, the Kingston by-pass, Box Hill and the coast.

The crack was brilliant between the owners of rival makes.
I started going there in late '61, when I had my Tiger 100 and I took a lot of barracking from the mob down there as it was a BSA and Norton stronghold during that time.

I had a bit more ammunition to use in the boasting, bragging, blarney and bullshit stakes once I'd got the Bonneville.

People would make up songs and chants, words fitted to popular tunes of the moment with which to taunt particular champions of other marques. One of which I'll include here for your dubious entertainment.

This should be sung, sweetly, in the Pub Singer's style.

To the tune of Teddy Bears Picnic.

If you go down the by-pass today you're in for a big surprise.
If you go down the by-pass today you'll never believe your eyes.
For all the Bonnies from miles around
Are gathered there, you should hear the sound
Today's the day the Bonnevilles have their buuuuurrrrn up.

Burn up time for Bonn-e-villes.
All the Bonn-e-villes are having a lov-er-ly burn today.
Winding past the Nor-or-tons
and thrashing all the BSAs.
Hammering down the Mickleham.
Heading for the kill.
The other bikes are out of date,
They just don't stand a chance.
Against a speed equipment Bonn-e-ville.

Git orf me barra
Against a speed equipment Bonn-e-ville.

Da - da - da - dum

As a factory option, duplex framed Bonnevilles could have the chopped monoblocks and a central, GP float bowl as on the '59s. It was listed under Speed Equipment and was only seen on a few road bikes.
A desirable tuning mod to an 18 year old, hell bent on local world highway speed records.

Making a statement in the continuous rivalry, Rob Smith pulled up on his new 650SS…. one Saturday afternoon…. people hanging out, just chatting.
He and his girlfriend Pauline dismounted strode across the wide pavement burst in the cafe and announced:

Alright Wells! Enough of this bullshit! Lights to the bridge now!

Rob was instigative in starting my motorcycling career; he'd borrowed a Norton and lent his Matchless G9 to my school mate and fellow Hot Rod and Gene Vincent fan Rick Harper.
Rick had a '32 Tudor when he was 19 then a 3 window '36. Just out of interest.
He lent me his Bantam and his licence and I was out on the road, on the way to Box Hill. Up to that point I wasn't in a rush to get a bike. I was 16 and had been around bikes but wanted a big old '30s American gangster car which some of the older kids had around my way. I had been out in a Hudson with some of them and that's what was in my mind.
That was until I got my motor running and got out on the highway. I know it was a 3 speed, 125 Bantam but the freedom it offered, the excitement and the danger that was available on every corner and roundabout was definitely an experience to be repeated and without a doubt because they'd already finished their teas by the time I got to Box Hill would have to be faster.

My Dad drove us down to Commerfords the following Saturday in his Consul and with the contents of my savings book £26 we bought a 1946 BSA XB32 iron 350 with battered chrome mudguards and the speedo in the tank. A bit too old fashioned looking by contemporary styles but it was a motorbike.

Commerfords delivered it with a new tyre fitted, as agreed and I set off in a red and black check donkey jacket, gauntlets and turned-down wellies.

No crash helmet.

My folks waved me off, they had never worn helmets, not many riders wore them.

When I bought my first helmet, a second-hand Racemaster which I painted red with yellow flames, I instantly became indestructible and immune from injury which led to my riding becoming even more reckless and fraught with risk taking.

I fell off or ran off the road on bends regularly during this period, trying to keep up with guys that had been riding a week or two longer than me.

My first ride with these kids was helmetless and was, without a doubt, the most terrifying experience of my motorcycling career so far.

The return spring on my kickstart broke and the lever hung down, nobody thought of tying the lever up and bumping the bike.

This is a bunch of 16 year olds with loads of enthusiasm and little knowledge or experience.

It was decided to tow me back home.

Somebody's washing line was volunteered and my Beeza was tied to the back of Eddy Earley's 500 Dominator.

Now as every motorcyclist knows; when being towed the rope should be round the steering head but loose and held by the hand on the handlebar in order to be able to let go of the rope and take a

different path should the towing bike get into difficulties or something goes wrong with the bike being towed.
We didn't know this and the rope was duly knotted onto both bikes.

I think Eddy just wanted to see how fast his Norton would go towing another bike.

It was bad enough down the Mad Mile, from the Banstead lights, my bike had never been that fast.
He was overtaking everything with me flapping about on the end of the rope.
There was no way I could get out of it or have any influence on the situation.
I was just hoping nothing terrible was going to happen.
He even pulled up, right at the front on the outside of the traffic at the Gander Green lights on the Sutton by-pass.
The driver of the car next to me must have seen the look of apprehensiveness on my face and kindly stayed still for Eddy to blast off in his drag race launch, snatching me off behind him regardless of the possibility of me getting squashed between the cars and the keep left sign.
One more speed record attempt bit of by-pass and we turn off and thread our way through some relatively slower roads.
I was well relieved to get untied at the end of it all.
I put on a nonchalant front because I thought this sort of experience was probably common to motorcyclists and my near blind panic was just because I was new to the game.
Why didn't you tie up the kickstart lever and bump start it. Said my Dad.

Doh! Said I.

Rob Smith had that year's model Super Rocket when he was 17. Chrome guards and two clocks. He talked a mate at work into signing the hire purchase agreement because his Dad wouldn't do it. Rob always wore the world's most worn out pair of wellies.
One day his Dad filled them up with water so he couldn't go out in them so he rode down to Brighton in his slippers.
He then had to bump start the bike due to a tied up kickstart lever, which required a fierce amount of toe and anus clenching to keep the slippers on during the side-saddle start.
He has an engineering firm on the Isle of Wight making bits and pieces for race cars, I see him now and again for a curry with other old pals from back then. It's always a laugh.

So three years later it's me and Rob, lights to the bridge on the Sutton by-pass heading north towards the Rosehill roundabout.
It was reckoned to be a quarter mile and the absolute test of who had the fastest bike.
The cafe emptied, a Zodiac filled up with boys and girls all laughing and joking squeezing in for a lift to the start to see the fun. Tony George joined us on his Constellation and Aussie Austin tagged along on his 110. This happened after my race at the Ace and I tried to explain how it was done there, when we all lined up on a green light. Yet when we got up to the lights Tony and Rob lined up on red and took off on amber.
I was back a few yards but went anyway and as luck would have it they were balked at a keep left sign with two cars, one making a turn left and I squirted past on the other side of them, the cars and the keep left sign, at about a 100; pulling over at the top sitting like Fonzi looking back down the road casually waiting for them.

Where've you been?

There's too much traffic here, we'll go down the Kingston.

's alright with me.

We pulled up at the South Lane lights no longer there on the Kingston by-pass.
They were after the Malden roundabout now a fly-under.
The Tolworth rise stretched out in front; a 6 lane dual carriageway with service roads either side running past the gardens of 30's suburban semis.
Apart from a couple of cars up the road apiece it looked like a drag strip.
We filtered down to the front of the 3 lanes of Sunday afternoon traffic waiting at the lights.
Pauline got off Rob's bike and sat down with her back to the traffic light pole.
Her handbag on her lap, looking up the road.

We are concentrating on the red light, clutches in and engines kicking up plenty of noise. There were probably some irate Daily Mail readers cursing us in their Sunday Standard 8s and probably some kids in the back of an old Zephyr cheering us.
We launched regardless and blasted up the empty road before us.
I had 112 by the crest of the rise, beating the new Norton 650SS with a two year old Bonneville.

Rob bought a Triton shortly after this.
My Bonnie was a 1960. Light blue and dark blue, I got it from Pride and Clarks part-exchanging my '55 Tiger 100 which I'd ridden unmercifully for 15 months.

By the time I traded in the old thing, it had Trophy pipes with a silencer made from a small copper fire extinguisher and I'd sawn the valence off the rear mudguard so it looked more like a Trophy.

Pride and Clarks was a business with two or three hundred bikes for sale all sizes solos and combinations, it was in Stockwell Road a Victorian canyon of tall terraced houses and big and little bike sales and repair shops. Prides had shops and showrooms on both sides of the road. All their buildings were painted red which really stood out in an inner city that had a general dull and dusky patina from all the coal fires and factories smoking away for centuries. They had their name in really big letters painted high up on the brickwork of the old buildings.

I had seen a Tangerine '59 there, in the morning when I was with Aussie who'd put a down payment on a black and white '59 Tiger 110.

The Bonnie was the cheapest one around at £150 but was not standing proud; it was slung against another bike.

It had scraped silencers, bent footrests and oil splattered all over the engine looking like it had been owned or stolen by a string of a hundred mile an hour everywhere lunatics.

It was the cheapest one ever at the time; I figured I could straighten it out and do it up.

My Dad to whom I had spoken very carefully was to lend me the rest of the money. I met him late afternoon in the showroom. He wouldn't even look at the '59.

You don't want that one.

He said, as he turned to look at a clean '60 that looked straight and proud.

There was only one other Bonnie there, a '61, out of hundreds of bikes in the shop.
Aussie and I had been to Commerfords and Elite Motors that morning, both looking for bikes, most big shops only had a few fast bikes amongst their vast stocks.
The '60 was £189, a tenner over the price I thought it was worth and I hadn't considered it but I wasn't going to argue.
A Bonneville was within my reach.
My Dad knew the salesman from before the war when they both worked at a bike shop called Motor Miles in Great Portland Street, where, he told me they had a lift to take the bikes up to the floor above and the showroom surfaces were such you could push the bikes into position, on their stands with your foot. He had driven a Harley float (a sidecar outfit for picking up bikes) for them and told a tale of how he used to broadside it around Trafalgar square, in the wet, on the slippery tarry-block surface.
He reminded the guy that he had once shared his sandwiches with him and got the part exchange upped a fiver, to 40 quid.

One hundred miles an hour came up in third on the straight along the bottom of Box Hill. The first time I'd ever seen it.
After a couple of years of trying to wring the ton out of a plunger 500 ZB Gold Star and a Tiger 100, melting pistons on a regular basis and only getting a best of 97 downhill with a tail wind, there it was effortlessly, on the speedo.
I knocked it into top, well pleased seeing that needle go past the 100 and followed Pete Simmonds on his Rocket at 105 until we turned off to go up to the café at the top of Box Hill.

I had a hundred in third down there.
Why didn't you come past me then?

I will next time.

Bomber was there on his Rocket, Bill Brown on his '60 CSR Sportstwin with DMD fairing.
They were nutters.
They would over take on a blind bend or a hump back bridge when the race was on.
Pete's Rocket had clip-ons right down the bottom and he seldom wore a helmet.
I once saw him unscrew a light bulb in the Caprice and stick his fingers in the bulb holder, for long enough to give a normal man a belt or twelve.
He was an electrician and had picked up a few tricks.
He just stood there and laughed as the lights flickered.
I saw him again recently and reminded him of it.
He said it really hurt.

It was decided to have a no-engine race down the pre speed bump Zig Zags, a narrow serpentine road on the side of Box Hill, back to the by-pass.
My bike was rolling well. I was about to pass Pete when he bumped started his engine, cutting it out again when he'd put enough distance between him and me.
A not very sporting trick indeed and yet one which I once had to employ when about to be passed by a Norton P11 in a similar race a dozen years later, in the Oakland hills.

Some of those guys in California could really chuck a bike about.

I knew this fellah called Doug, he played fiddle in The Starry Plough on Shattuck in Berkeley. Shit-kicking, hillbilly music.
This would be '73-'74.

He had a KR model Harley that he'd found lying on its side in an orchard and had bought for 75 bucks.
He'd ridden it across the country 3 times and told me that one time just outside of Deadman's Gulch; the headwind was so strong that even going downhill he'd had to drop a cog to keep up some kind of forward motion.
He'd fitted a Triumph conical front end and a plain black, slim Triumph tank.

I did that just to piss off the Harley owners. He laughed.

He was so quick up the landscaped, winding roads through the residential Berkeley Hills; Kenny Roberts would have had a hard job to stay with him.

Talking about fast riders...

One day whilst hanging out in the lay-by that was once half way down the Leatherhead bound straight of the Mickleham by-pass at the bottom of Box Hill and a regular stop on a Sunday afternoon, I saw a Triumph on the other carriageway, go by quicker than most. It meant he'd come around the bends promptly in order to make such a fast pass of the lay-by.
It was dark red and silver, that year's Trophy colours.

That's Dave Degens.

He's not hanging about.

That was the first time I heard that name, a name soon to be famous for winning the 24 hour race at Barcelona on his Triton and for building a legion of Tritons.

Later in life he told me he could get round those bends at 100. That was fast.
I have got to put my hands up. I was never that quick but I did get round them fast enough to be clocking 100 as I came out of them and still frighten myself in the meantime.

Right then keep it down to 60.

Ok. 60 it is.

Yeah.

Everyone nodded, sort of.
Knowing deep down that there was very little chance of that ever being the case.
At least it had been said.

This was agreed as oft times before one day when setting out for Brighton on one of my first rides with the wave of highway delinquents that featured when I first started hanging out at the Caprice.
It was like the warm up lap, sliding through the traffic on the way to the beginning of St Helier Avenue, a dual carriageway that ran up through the estate.
As soon as we hit the dual carriageway it was off, a mad blat all doing 90s coming up to the roundabout at Rose Hill then more of the same down the Sutton by-pass.
Something would bring an air of calm over the proceedings and the pace would slow for a few miles until some other bikes were encountered and the tear-arsing would start up again.

The scene was evolving all the time and the more you rode with the same guys the safer it got.
So you could know where anyone was at any moment of the ride and also what he would be likely to do in any situation.
The one time Tony George didn't do what I thought he would do resulted in us not having a terrible great pile up.
It was like there was divine intervention or something along those lines.
It happened on the day of the photo of the bikes lined up at the Mote caff just North of Pulborough on the A29. We had just got back on the road and the speeds had built up so that after the staggered junction at Pulborough everyone was full on caning it. I was winding it up through the gears, to catch up after getting snagged behind some vehicles and rounded a bend to find Tony overtaking a line of cars.
Another line of cars came the other way and left a narrow gap which on any other occasion he would have charged through.
I was braking hard and skidding but going too fast to stop and would have hit him right up the tail light, spreading us all over the road and into and under the oncoming cars.

I did see a Tiger 110 hit Ronnie Lovegrove's Trophy hard up the tail pipe while we were all going for it, down the white line, in Sunday afternoon traffic, on the A217 at the top of Reigate Hill. He held onto his Trophy with the wide bars. The 110 with clip-ons was spread all over the road. The rider, unconscious with a broken arm, ended up on the pavement, luckily not under a car.
During the drama a big irate motorist appeared and had a fit, screaming and shouting at us. Ronnie stood there, patiently looking up at the guy ranting on about the way we were riding and we knew he had a point but he was only making matters worse. Ron waited for the guy to take a breath, looked him straight in the eyeballs and

told him to Foxtrot Oscar. Which he did. It was a good choice of words and an air of calm returned to the proceedings as we waited for the ambulance.
None of that Mitcham lot ever wore helmets.
Ronnie Lovegrove had a choice '56 TR6 that would do 115 and he looked like a cross between Jack Palance and the Fonz.

For some reason Tony tucked into the gap between the cars on our side just far enough to allow me to let off the brakes and go through the gap between the cars in front of him.
I thought it was a miracle.

He just said. These things happen.

Tony had a mention in the Evening Standard and the Daily Mail for a spectacular crash on a Bonneville that took place one Sunday morning on St Helier Avenue.
We had spent the night with two lovely sisters, Lorraine and Linda in someone's parents' house, looking right out on the actual road.
I claimed the record down the Avenue, at that time. 108.
Tony set out, that morning helmetless wearing just his suit and a collar and tie from the night before to beat the record. It was about 9 o'clock and he said he was doing 115 as he went by the house.
We were watching from an upstairs window to see a Jowett Javelin pull out of a side road and quickly take position in the right hand lane to turn through a gap in the central reservation. Tony was overtaking another car and didn't see it until he was on it.
He hit the brakes, the forks went down.
He hit the car on its right rear corner.
I saw the bike go into a fierce tank-slapper then disappear behind the Jowett.

I grabbed my jacket and put it on as I ran across the greens towards the wreck to see if there was anything that could be done.

The Bonnie was stuck up the curb of the central divider and resting up against a disused, cast iron post of a keep left sign from a previous decade. The tank and one exhaust pipe and silencer were amongst the motorcycle parts debris scattered in a long trail from the point of contact.

Tony was nowhere to be seen.

I scanned the environs; people were looking out from their upstairs windows.

Some were talking to a paper boy who pointed to the roundabout, a couple of hundred yards away.

I looked down there and saw a figure, lurking, loping and limping between the bushes.

Sprinting to the roundabout, I found Tony, blood running out of everywhere, his suit ripped to ribbons.

He had no shoes or socks and wanted to leave immediately.

We limped, dragged and staggered back, in as clandestine a way as was possible in broad daylight, to the house where the girls did their best to dress his wounds but we did stand out a bit for a Sunday morning.

Everyone had noticed.

The police had been called.

There was no escape and he needed a hospital.

He was captured and sure enough, did pay his debt to society.

Things like this do happen. Tony was lucky to get away without breaking anything too serious. A mob of us went to visit him in hospital, getting told off by matron for all the larking about.

There were a few crashes and near misses and lucky escapes.

Vic Willoughby, who had a '60 Bonnie, was killed at night round the Surrey Arms bend, a local bend with a smooth surface.

Everybody took that bend fast, in both directions. Something went wrong. The stand dug in and lifted the back wheel or the tyre gave out, anyway he slid across the road into a head-on with an oncoming car.
The funeral was very sad, lots of tears from the many boys and girls he knew.

I remember, back then, feeling that I would live forever and anyway if I died my story would be told down the cafe for years to come.
A Gung Ho feeling that was felt by many.
We weren't really rebelling, just doing what came naturally and anyway you couldn't fail to have respect for the previous generation as they'd been in a world war. They'd either been up to their necks in muck and bullets in a foreign land or had bombs falling on their houses or factories, hospitals and pubs in their own backyard.
We were the first generation not to have to do National Service. The first to have the full on teenage experience. Like in West Side Story when the old boy who runs the cafe says to a Jet: When I was your age . . . and the kid says: My age? You was never my age!

The authorities were always a problem but they've always been tricky to deal with even before the Romans got here.

One night in that bad winter of '62-'63 a few of us were riding down the Kingston by-pass, the mucky and frozen snow was swept into banks either side of the carriageway, leaving nearly two out of the three lanes open. The traffic had bunched up and I waited just behind the corner of a car for a chance to pass.
We'd been riding fast all the way from Morden and I was hovering there because there was only about 12 inches of road between the cars' tyres and the frozen snow and I didn't fancy getting on the ice.

There was an explosion from the pipes of Ernie Parrish's Triumph and snow and ice flying everywhere as he went round the outside of me and the car, shooting past on the lumpy, banked-up ice. About 80 mph.
A truly heroic manoeuvre especially as his Bonnie had clip-ons, right down low and push bike lights. Cliff Rushworth has Ernie's '60 Bonneville today. It's beautifully restored with new old stock, factory tanks and mudguards.

We were on our way to a bike meet in a shack somewhere, just off the Kingston by-pass at the Toby Jug. Ginger McRae reminded me that it was called River Hill Riders.
It was run by a motorcycle cop that did his best to try and improve the riding of this young generation of motorcyclists, who were getting a lot of bad press of late.
The 59 club was going but never really appealed because it was on the other side of London and it was run by a Vicar.
This was a blast down the Kingston and somewhere to go on a winter's Thursday night. Quite a few young bikers got there, even some from right out in the sticks. One guy told us he'd been done for poaching.
A TV company did turn up one night and filmed us hanging out there and riding off down the snow covered track. Martin told me he and some others were filmed riding to Brighton. He said the film company was Canadian and the film was called Coffee Bar Racers. A bunch of us got to watch it at the Teddington studios.
It looked like news footage of cold motorcycling.
The club was well run we did a good bike quiz, watched short films and were advised on safe riding.

One time, after launching into a monologue about the terrible liberties some bikers take, the cop began to illustrate his points with

an anecdote as an example of the outrageous riding he had witnessed.
He said to the assembled mob of young herberts sat, thawing out on wooden chairs, in all their slightly unfurled, winter bike clobber.

I have stood at the South Lane lights, on the Kingston by-pass on a Sunday afternoon.

And some bright spark said:

With a starters flag!

Everybody roared with laughter. It was hilarious.

We only went a few times, there was usually something going on around Morden.
Johnsons was a great cafe. It was always a motorcycle cafe.
My family had been hop pickers and we were drawn to Kent, on a sunny Sunday, as often as the south coast.
My folks used to call in there on the outfit, when I was just knee high to a whippersnapper.
It was on a straight stretch with a rise either side of it, just past Brands on the old A20.
A detached, single story transport cafe purpose built, on a budget before the war.
Nothing much either side of it and greenery opposite.

Parked out front, facing the road were the big guns, the polished Goldies, stripped down Nortons and sawn-off Super Rockets. Short mudguards chrome springs racing seats ally rims.
One I remember was a duplex framed Bonneville with a narrow, hand crafted polished aluminium, full fairing, covering the front

wheel. No lights, an ally tank, a red frame and a copper plated back hub.
He had the initials JL on the tank along with a line of little bombs painted like aircrew did on their warplanes.
I took it to mean the number of top guns he'd burned off.
One guy had a raced-up '60 110 with Gunga Din written on the tank.
Along the sides and out back were bikes of the lesser leagues, the odd one with dubious origins or ex-racers and specials that didn't have stands.
I did get to see JL, with the ally faring, run at Duxford, later on and he was quick.
The word was a guy brought a Vincent down to Johnsons one day, in a van and did take his crown out on the road.

One Sunday, the BMW crowd, 4 or 5 older dudes all in black leathers with their bikes parked up on the little bit of tarmac footpath in front of the forecourt, stood chatting, shooting the breeze.

I really don't know what they like about BMWs. I declared to Paul Cole.

They're queers' bikes he concluded.

It seemed an amusing assumption.

Death Hill or The Gorse, the council kept changing its sign.
Sometimes pronounced: The Goss.
It was the stretch of the A20, London direction, down from Brands, where best to achieve an optimum top speed and to be able to get

round Suicide, the bend at the bottom before the roundabout, at a 100 was only for the brave and the mad.
The only graffiti on the wall of the medieval urinal, out back of the cafe, were claims of speed and challenges. One said:

>MY TIGER 110
>120 DOWN THE GOSS
>123 ABC his reg number..

Another said:

>MY GOLD STAR
>DEATH HILL 125
>ABC 123

The place had a great vibe to it, a serious road race feeling to the proceedings.

Back at the Caprice in Morden the fun and games went on as usual. Including the hit and run acquisition of tube train ticket inspector's hats that would be duly bent up to try and get them to look like, what were referred to as, Harley hats, as seen worn by riders in early American bike pictures.
Somehow they ended up having a slight Gestapo air about them. They had their moments but they wouldn't stay on at speed and most days you got involved in a race somewhere and it wasn't a good idea to have to mess about with a hat under race conditions. Mostly they were worn for extreme posing, in the early days.

We're all guilty. To one degree or another.

Martin Small, John Willers and I set off one Saturday evening from the Caprice to do Chelsea Bridge, The Ace and The Busy Bee. Martin had the 600 Dominator featured in some of the pics.

John had the Vincent/Norton.
He built this bike in his backyard shed where he had a lathe and other well used engineering tools.
John had done a bit of grass track racing and this was the first bike he had on the road.
It got to be on the cover of Motorcycle Mechanics and was in 1964 on the Solvol Autosol stand at the Earls Court bike show for the next year's models.
John went on to form ARE (Alloy Racing Equipment) and make 750 conversions for Triumphs then start the firms Accessory Mart and Domi-Racer in the States.
I see Martin on the Caprice Club curry nights. He is well laid back and we both remember stuff the other had forgotten.

We rode up into London past all the tube stations and across Clapham Common to drop down to the Bridge, had a cup of tea; it was early, there were only a couple of bikes parked in the kerb. The summer nights there were great, loads of bikes about, people arriving with their eyes streaming, like they'd been doing a hundred miles an hour on the way there.
Blokes trying to get the hundred from the roundabout to the bridge. Bikes pulling away fast, the ones with a close box winding out first gear into the far off night time distance.

The hot dog stall on Chelsea Bridge was a frontier outpost on the wrong side of the border between the West End-Kensington-Chelsea conurb and the dark satanic mills of Nine Elms and Battersea.
Even so it was double cool at the Bridge, only the best on parade; Gold Stars, Super Rockets, all the Triumphs, Nortons and everything else.
Two old dressed Harleys got up there sometimes.

They were the only Harleys I'd ever seen about London and the south.
They were ridden by two older couples who all wore old American leather jackets, with the white pleat inserts, and proper Harley hats with the white peaks
These folk were from some earlier Beat, James Dean, Kerouac generation and they looked like they had celebrated their bikes and their style forever.
All four of them were small scale, neat and they complimented their machines real well.
One time they were at the big café at Hickstead, on the Brighton Road.
There were loads of bikes there; it was a sunny Sunday in summer. One guy with us said to one of the Harley guys, as they were mounting up:

What do you use these for? Caravan work?

The old dudes and their women just laughed, kicked the bikes into life, pulled and pressed a few levers and pedals and the two old American dinosaurs moseyed gracefully through the forecourt and off down the sunny road to Brighton.

I had stopped and looked in Fred Warr's window, in New Kings Road. It was a real olde worlde bike shop back then. Wooden counter and floors with one Sportster and one 'Glide for sale.
I love the older Harleys now but couldn't see the attraction in those days. I reckoned there was nothing better than a 650 Triumph for all urban, by-pass and coast route applications.

One night Graham Carlton and I arrived at the Bridge to find no bikes just a couple or three police cars and a couple of motorcycle cops.
We pulled into the closed entrance to Battersea Park, bang opposite the dog stall and being aware of all the beady eyes watching us, made the turn to go back the way we came.
A motorcycle cop followed us and pulled us over.

Where you from? He's sitting on his bike, next to me, engine running.

Morden.

What are you doing up here.

We've come up for a tea.

He looked away then looked back.

If I see you up here again tonight, doing 30, I'll nick you for 50 and if you are doing 40 I'll nick you for 70 with no lights. ……
FUCK OFF.

Charming. We thought and duly fucked off out of it. Not that we were going to hang about anyway with all that lot lurking with intent.
Who, we wondered, wanted the hot dog stall to themselves that night?
This is the big bad city and there are some dangerous fuckers about.

On the way back, pulling away from the lights at Tooting Bec and showing off to some giggling girls in a Mini, we ended up doing a

100 down an empty Tooting High Street. Two coppers who were looking in Dorothy Perkins window, heard us coming and walked into the road and waved torches at us as we went by.
We couldn't hang about, we had a lot on.

From the Bridge we headed west to pick up the North Circular.
On a dual carriageway near Hammersmith just as we were going smartly into a roundabout, two police Thunderbirds shot by us, a bit lively and dived into the roundabout as if they were heading off to the right.
The roundabout was high with builder's boards so that you couldn't see which road they'd taken.
We all came out of the roundabout right on the speed limit.
We checked with each other but we'd all tumbled their game.
They came flying up behind us only to find three young, highway scallywags with painted helmets and leather jackets, riding out and out raced up bikes, all doing exactly 30 miles an hour, in single file.
They rode alongside and looked our bikes over, for bloody ages.
John's Norvin always attracted attention.
We all kept our eyes on the road ahead.
Everything must have looked impressive enough because they rode off.
After making sure they weren't going to turn up behind us again we went back to riding at normal, excessively fast speeds up to the Ace, where we had another tea then set off for the Busy Bee.

The Bee was deserted that night. The only time I went there. Maybe there was a big party on, somewhere else or something.
I was hoping to find somebody, who might have helped me out with a wheel bearing, seeing as I'd had one collapse on the way over.
I was flat out behind John's NorVin.
It was the first and only time I saw 120. 7000 in top.

I swear I was catching him but the road was interrupted by a roundabout and we had to ease off.

As I was braking, at about 60 mph, the right hand, tapered bearing in the rear wheel broke up and the wheel came off the QD splines in the brake drum and was flopping about on the spindle.

We rode home slowly, the wheel popped out a few times but I popped it back in and got the bike home. John took me to a mates place to borrow a wheel for the next day.

I was clinging onto that wheel and tyre, sitting on the hump of that Norvin's racing seat with no footrests, at 100 mph from South Wimbledon to Morden.

It did sound well in the still of that summer's night and it was a risk well worth taking in order not to miss out on Sunday's action at Box Hill.

Bernies was a cafe that featured for a bit. It was in the dip, on that same stretch of road between South Wimbledon and Morden as is the pub where the Mighty South London Triumph owners club meet, on occasion. The Prince of Wales.

Messengers was an all night cafe at the South Wimbledon lights. Pie and beans with lashings of brown sauce was served 24 hours a day in the tiny black and white tiled diner. There was always someone in there at any time of the night and old boys could doss in the back if they had nowhere else to go.

There was a giant shiny steel tea urn on the counter and sometimes a Vincent Black Prince, the fared one, parked on the pavement, outside. I never knew the owner was the woman that worked there in the afternoons.

I found out years later, talking to a guy with a Bonneville I met at the Hand in Hand on the side of Wimbledon Common, Pete

Charlton that it was his Mother's Vincent and she had owned Messengers.

Just across the road from Messengers, at the South Wimbledon lights, another cafe began staying open at night.
I was in there, one evening, suited, with Lorraine and her sister Linda and Tony Latham. There was a guy playing the pinball that I was about to get to know.
He had 'T.110, Bonneville, Special, 650' painted on the back of his jacket along with some other stuff that I took to be an out and out challenge.
In the kerb was a highly polished, chrome and blue, single down tube Triumph with a Bonnie head and clip-ons and rear-sets.
I explained to Lorraine that I had no choice. I had to go home and get my bike.
She moaned but I saw her smile.
I jumped on the tube, one stop and was back at the cafe pronto.
They were waiting on the pavement as I pulled up.
Quick! He went that a way.
I blasted off, checking the main side roads.
I saw his tail light turn a corner; he was flying about the back streets. I hammered it, hot on the trail and pulled up level with him, in the middle of the road.
He was sat on his bike, talking to a girl, stood on the pavement with her arms folded under her breasts. He wore no helmet and his lank hair hung, long, down the sides of his face.
He stopped talking to her when I pulled up.
He looked at my bike and then at me.
I nodded down the road, by way of noble challenge.
He said something to his girlfriend, leaned over on the clip-ons, took a confident swing on the kick start and the motor barked into life with a strong, fresh metal proclamation.

He knocked it into gear.
Off he went, as fast as you like.
Running a red light, at speed, at South Wimbledon lights.
I'd never seen this guy before.
He was a full-on nutter and he was up for a balls-out scorch through the traffic down to the Kingston by-pass where our riding skills, bike performance and risk taking, on a blat to the Scilly Isles and back, were very evenly matched.
Back in South Wimbledon, we parked up in the warm summer's night air and chatted about the bikes.
It was Barry, a good man with the spanners and great laugh.
He lived off Merton High Street and had just finished building his bike from a tumble-down shed full of Triumph parts at the bottom of his mum's little garden.
He married his girlfriend and went to New Zealand.
Well. What are you gonna do, there wasn't much on the tele in those days.

MODS AND ROCKERS

They're Modernists. Someone said in my ear as we watched three fellahs do a tour of the walkway which was lined by columns, around the outside of the dance floor of the Wimbledon Palais. It was a good sized place, where, of a summers evening, there would be Gold Stars, Rockets, Trophys, Tiger 110s, Sportstwins, Dominators parked rear wheel in, in the side road, in the glow of the neon of the entrance and big, old yanks turning up, particularly from Sutton and Worcester Park.
Buicks with side mounted spare wheels.
Buicks with buck teeth.
One of those fellahs had an early thirties Cadillac tourer with gangster whitewalls.

Loads of kids digging the scene with a Rock and Roll lean.

There were two stages at the Palais, one either side of the dance floor, a surround of tables and chairs, a column lined walkway around all of that and a bar at each end.
This is 1960. No alcohol on Saturday afternoons and Tuesday evenings.
All the best music.
Early teenage stuff.
The Tooting boys and everyone from up that way stood to one side of the big stage and Mitcham and Wimbledon stood on the other.
There was a territorial theme to where and how you stood and walked.
There was courtship cool jiving. Nothing fancy.

Not much violence.
There was a bit of a row in the street, out front of the Palais, one Saturday afternoon.
The fight involved 7 or 8 young geezers.
It took place in amongst the Saturday afternoon traffic.
There were even blokes battering one another all over the old, unloved motor bikes that always stood waiting for new owners, on the pavement outside Abbey Spares.
Generally, though, the place had a good vibe, charged with jiving on the sprung dance floor and the promise of teenage kicks all through the night.

These Modernists wore black leather, suit style, two button jackets, new Levis with no turn ups and loafers.
What are they all about? Somebody said.
Within a week or so we ended up all becoming mates, through mutual friends. We generally cut capers and had a laugh. The sort of kids that would bunk in the cinema and never buy a train ticket but would give up their seat on a bus, to a woman with shopping.
These Modernists were Bill Thurston, Bob Parsons and Tall Alan Cowland. They were from Palestine Grove, Merton Abbey, a now forgotten neighbourhood, across the River Wandle, out back of the Palais and they listened to the likes of Charlie Parker and Charlie Mingus.
Our lot all wore Italian drapes with the high neck and 4 or more buttons. The velvet collars were long gone around my way.
I gave the jazz a listening-to but stuck with Rock and Roll.

My roots were established.
The first record I bought was Bluejean Bop. It was a toss-up between that and Heartbreak Hotel but that was in the Hit Parade

and you heard it now and again on the dull, old, Wilfred Pickles and Worker's Playtime, '50s British radio.
I read the headlines, early in the morning, as a paper boy, when Buddy Holly was killed.
I saw Gene Vincent in 1959, at the Tooting Granada, now the most luxurious bingo hall in the world.
It was built, Egyptian temple style, by a famous German architect, in the '30s, with columns, statues and arches.
Gene was dressed in a cool American shirt and strides of the time.
This is a couple of months after Jerry Lee was kicked out of the country for breaking the written rule.
Apart from two gigs Jerry Lee played before he was shown the door, Gene was the first American Rock and Roll star to perform in England.
The audience knew this and they also knew that the current British stuff didn't come up to muster.
They showed their appreciation.
Gene was world class.
The audience, all youth, loads of haircuts and drapes and good looking chicks called for encore after encore.
As it happened the chant of 'We want Gene' prevented Marty Wilde from doing his set, as top of the bill.
He appealed but the chant couldn't be stopped. It was a wild old night.

The first time I heard the word Rocker was in autumn '62. Before the newspapers got hold of the word and fanned the flames of teenage tribal rivalries.
Airsey aka the Colonel and I had ended up in Thetford one Saturday night in his old '40s Vauxhall.

We had driven there because it seemed that no-one from around our way had ever been to Norfolk and we thought it might turn into an adventure.
In the early evening we called in at a cafe that looked like, maybe, there was something going on.
There were a few locals about and a little posse of young geezers from East Ham, working away from home for a bit.
They had college boy haircuts, the current mod style, short Italian jackets and jeans.
We had longer barnets, black leather jackets and jeans.
A couple of them were funny and friendly. We mated up and all got on like a house on fire, telling jokes and stories of where we came from and what we'd been up to.
The whole lot of us squeezed into the Vauxhall and went to a shindig in an abandoned mansion.
Bee Bumble and the Stingers played.
They were a good band, even if they did do Nutrocker one too many times.
We had a great night and shook hands at the end of it like old pals.

I knew the word would be coined but I hadn't formed it myself.
The world was changing.
The sixties started in '63, the time of The Beatles and The Stones and the visiting American Blues men.
Before that it was the Fifties and some wanted to stay with the old style Teddy Boy clobber and Rock and Roll.
They were the Rockers.
Some of those guys liked bikes and they took on the title.
The East Ham lad who used the word to describe an old school friend that they all knew, paused, like he thought he'd spoken out of turn.
Like he thought it had a derogatory connotation.

It was cool. I knew exactly what was meant.

The Mods seemed to think the Rockers were behind the times but what did they know?

The Mods did outnumber the Rockers, for a bit. One wave of them were post war baby boomers and were growing in strength summer by summer.
Swarms of scooters would flood the highways.
They did have a look about them.
Especially that couple of weeks in one summer when they all wore those short baggy dayglow jeans with their parkas and Gabby Hayes hats.
Moving slowly, prrrrop-pop-popping in a pack, through an urban environment, all strutting their stuff with their paint and chrome.
In rude boy hats. Suited and booted.
Birds, posing like royalty, on the pillions, in Pac-a-Macs and Hush Puppies or whatever was the mode of the moment.

One Sunday afternoon I was winding up the rise, towards Leatherhead from the Mickleham bends. It was great to hit the roundabout, at the top, at speed as it has a nice dip that you could dive into as you cut the corners. Even if there was a bit of traffic about it was often possible to get round it fast, if you judged it right. This particular time I came flying on to the roundabout and found a gaggle of G.Ss and Lambrettas, dawdling, like whoever was leading was deciding which road to take.
There is really only one way. The other one is a back lane.
I could see a channel through all the scooters and there must have been a dozen of them.

I managed to do the roundabout at the same speed that I could have done it if it was clear. Flicking it through the scooters, flat out with loads of roaring from my open pipes.
It must have made them jump. I mused, as I wound it up through the gears, that I'd left them all wobbling about and banging their bubbles together like plastic ducks in a fairground barrel.
Waving their fists.

My inevitable retribution followed a bit later, that summer in 1962.
I was with some mates riding into Brighton and got stuck behind some Mods riding past Preston Park on the way in.
I just couldn't sit behind them and crept past them at 1 mph faster than their dead on 30.
There was a white shirted police inspector and a constable stood outside a police box on the other side of the road, opposite a side road.
I couldn't back off. I was committed.
I was on the outside of a school of scooters and would have had to ride along behind them to stay within the limit.
Just couldn't arrive in Brighton under those conditions.
The gods of rock'n'roll had decreed this somewhere in my ancestral memory.
I looked the main copper in the eye as I went past.
He looked back at me and he didn't look happy.
In the side road I saw a black, police Flash parked with rider.
Looking behind I saw him pull out and knew he was after me.
I backed off to below 30.
The bloody scooters went by as I slowed to 25 and he eventually pulled me.
He did me for 42.
I begged him to let me go as I already had three endorsements and one more would surely mean a loss of licence.

I gave it my best and he did weaken a bit but said he'd been told to nick me by Herr Inspector.
As it happened, in the end, it cost me a fiver with three pounds costs and a further endorsement.
I was well pleased, I still had my licence.

A while later, by way of revenge I did a 100 along that bit, on the way out of town.

Coincidentally I'd been nicked there on my first bike for no L plates, carrying a passenger and speeding and just to show how dumb I really am, I was pulled over and nearly done on the same stretch in the '90s when I rode down there the day of the Pioneer run.
Circumstances allowed my reprieve.
It must be something about that bit of road.
Nowadays when I come into Brighton for the Rockers Run or the Sprint, I ride in from the Shoreham end, along the prom.
Keeping an eye out for the cameras.

Johnny Sullivan got done twice for speeding, in two different counties on the same night when we were camping in North Wales.

We'd sent the tent to Colwyn Bay on the train and ridden up there.
Dizzy Evans's back brake on his 110 gave up the ghost on the way there.
It had smoke billowing from it at one point and it didn't work after that.
Then the day we went to Snowdonia and had ridden way up high in the hills, his front brake cable snapped.
We all had Triumphs but they all had different cable set-ups so we couldn't swap one over on to Diz's bike.

It was decided that he should take it easy, on the way back down the mountain. There was hardly any traffic about and if he used the gears to slow himself down he would probably be alright.

It was alright, for quite a long way down those stone wall sided roads, past the odd slate roofed cottage and through all that stone walled countryside.

That is, until rounding a bend, hidden by walls and cliff sides in the middle of nowhere, there was a bus stopped unloading and loading passengers.

It was a narrow road and a Morris Minor had stopped to chat with the driver, leaving too narrow a gap for a bike between itself and the bus and barely enough room on the left side of the road, by the wall.

I stopped and looked apprehensively back up the road.

John saw it, as he rounded the bend he gave a look of horror at the thought of the impending drama and pulled up by the wall.

Diz came around the corner, took in the situation, in a flashing of wagging head and eyes and decided the safest way was through on the right hand side of the road between the bus and the wall. The side where all the women were unloading shopping and nattering by the back door of the bus.

He'd crashed down through the gearbox but disappeared from view behind the bus, a bit too fast, shouting with a meaningful expression on his face:

LOOK OUT!

Jesus it could have been terrible but miraculously he went right through the lot of them and came out the other side without any major harm being done.

I think he had a mouthful of cornflakes, the front page of the local paper draped across his chest and maybe a leak up his jumper from when all the shopping went flying up in the air.
Casting a fleeting glance at the devastation, we skedaddled, amongst hollers, shouts and curses from the disarrayed victims and luckily got back to the campsite without further ado.
Picking up a cable the next day, at a bike shop in Rhyll.

John lost and retrieved a silencer on the M1, on the way back to London and on the North Circular in traffic, I looked back to see Diz's engine pumping out oil in spurts from the hole where the dynamo used to live.
This was a £50, '54 Tiger One One O from Pride and Clarks and after a rebuild and many a road mile, Diz eventually built it into a drag bike that he christened Loki, after the Viking god of mischief.
I had a go on it, in its early days, at Duxford, just in the pit area and it was quick.
Diz lived up the road from me, I knew him from 10 years of age, his Dad died in the war and he lived in a nice yet impoverished house with his Mum and sister.
As soon as he got a job at 15 he bought a burned out, from the screen back, '46 Cadillac for £8, he was going to restore it.
Unfortunately when it was delivered they put the shiny front end facing inwards on the drive. The rear was red rusty with no glass.
It did look sore and sat there for ages.
His Mum, eventually, made him get rid of it and he bought a '37 V8 Ford sedan, then he had the urge for a motorbike and got the 110.

Getting back to the early days of Mods and Rockers; the scene was changing. I rode with some guys, one Sunday in late '63, mates of mates, there was an outfit with us and the twat in the sidecar was

breaking off car aerials as they hazardously wove their way, along the white line, through the traffic.
This is in Cobham, a small Surrey Town.
He was a prat and he didn't even have a bike.
It was a sign of the times to come.

There were thugs about doing horrible things during these years, for sure but Rockers were usually busy doing stuff with their machines; stipping them down to get the race bike look, straightening out crash damage and rebuilding and tuning engines. Round my way there were no older kids with bikes that could pass on a few tips from their experience. There were a few clues from some Dads but generally we were just figuring it out as we went along with help from folklore and hearsay. This was a totally consuming thing. Violent conflict with other bikers was not on the agenda during this episode of the culture. The only anti-social activity was tearing about fast everywhere and making a lot of noise. The kids I knocked about with all had a heart and have all turned out to be decent blokes.

Yet time was marching on.
The unit Bonneville had arrived looking like the pre-unit's quieter and more responsible brother.
They even painted it in Holier than Thou white.
The bike companies always tried to play down the excitement on the home market models. The US bikes looked so much better.
The Gold Star went out of production also the Rocket Gold Star which was a gallant stand, at the end of that era.

Winter was coming; little Rhythm and Blues bands were playing in little dance halls out the back of pubs which incidentally were full of crumpet.

I had my car licence and figured I was nearly 20 and it was time to settle down and move in to the car and pub world, proper.
In late '63 I had my Bonnie painted in polychromatic bronze in H.E Greens' bicycle shop, just along from the Caprice and had bits like the mudguard stays and number plate bracket chromed.
An impulse to get a Zodiac got hold of me one day and I sold the bike to Elite Motors. Then owned a series of interesting motors that I tore about in and had my share of lucky crashes in, for 18 months before it was decided, with Ray McCormack, whilst sat in an empty pub, one wet winter's weekday night, to set off around the world in a 15cwt Thames van.

I rambled the earth for a few years, mainly travelling back and forth to India then the US. Owning a bike here and there until I reconnected with the motorbike world when I walked down to the end of the road from the house that I'd been taken to, the night before in Oakland.
That would be after driving across the country, from New York with Sue and her son Auri, who were moving to L.A.
There I met Mary Lou, camping, in Leo Carrillo (Pancho in The Cisco Kid) State Park, north of Santa Monica.
We had just spent a few days driving up The Pacific Coast Highway in her Beetle with her daughter Stacy.
She lived in a house with two other, beautiful, women.

Right opposite the end of her road, on Telegraph Avenue, was a British bike shop. The Grease Pit, later to revert to the firm's original title; GP Cycle Works.
I got to know these guys.
It was great to be around bikers again and British bike fans as well. It was run by Rick Price. He was about 25 and had been in the British bike business since he bought his first Triumph at 17.

They started in a shed and had been in the shop a couple or three years. Nowadays Rick and GP are in Sacramento.
They were busy back then; three mechanics, all lunatics:
Frank, a car club bloke from South San Francisco, he drove a '68 Charger over the Bay Bridge every day. He had one blue eye and one brown eye.
He said one was for Triumph and the other was for BSA.
There was Rick's original mate, Steve who left for Europe and John Greynald aka Squeeky John who'd had the first motorized skateboard in L.A.
He told me a story about one time when he was working at Bud Ekins's place and a guy stuck his head in the workshop and said: Elvis has just walked in!
All the mechanics came out of the workshop to have a look at the King and his entourage.
They were all tickled pink.
Elvis and his pals bought 10 Triumphs.
Trophys, Bonnies, TT Specials.

Thang you very murch.

U'hu

One day, I was out on my '56 TR6 with Frank, on a 4 cylinder Indian, Rick on a Rocket Three and John on his bored out 350 Honda with clip-ons and rear-sets.
We'd taken a ride along the lovely winding roads north of the Golden Gate and back into the City.
Frank was showing us some of the steeper view points, up in San Francisco's hills.
We came to a 4 way stop, way up high and all four of us are lined up waiting for our turn to go.

You couldn't see where the road opposite, across the intersection went to because it dropped away.
Not unusual around these parts but this one dropped away more than any other.
Frank had seen this happen before; you could tell by the way he laughed.
We all took off quick but John did a drag race start, right across the intersection.
He went airborne off the edge and must have done two thirds of the block at least ten feet up in the air. Landing and braking in a hanging over the handlebars, hopping about, fish-tailing skid before the criss-cross traffic at the next intersection.
How we chuckled at his folly.

Rick ran a tight ship. Always packed heat, having one time, been robbed at gunpoint on the pavement, outside the shop. He played guitar and liked a laugh.
He did pick up some huge British bike part inventories, Triumph and BSA, from guys in the surrounding Californian towns that had them from years before, when they'd sold bikes.
The Grease Pit had tons of stuff.
It was just a small shop in a once Italian, still had a fantastic deli, but predominantly black neighbourhood.
Pretty cool, just a couple of girls working out of a small motel and not too much gunfire.

On first seeing the place I popped in and asked if there was any fear of a start but didn't get a job right then.
I was wearing Prince of Wales check trousers and braces, probably looking like a mini-cab driver that had spent 14 days in an open boat.

He offered me a job 6 months later when I went in for a brake cable for my Trophy and by which time I'd learned some of their California ways.
I was the parts man, behind the counter with an English accent. Surely he must know what he's talking about. I hoped they'd think.
I had a wind-up call one day from a guy wanting to build a Triton, an exotic British special he'd heard about.
He had a single down tube Triumph frame and 500 Norton twin engine, from a Dominator 7.
I was very polite and explained the preferred choice of components. I should have twigged at the time that it was a wind-up, probably something to do with Ken Seavey and Tom Davenport, a couple of stone British bike freaks that I got to know and will have get the truth out of them when I eventually bump into them again.

Ken liked a Matchless, having discovered scramblers in Arizona. He owned one and a half G45s, a G50 with lights, with his mate Tugboat John and rode a G12 CSR with his unserviceable right arm draped on the right handlebar, held in place by the bar end mirror. The brake, clutch and the throttle, which turned the other way, were on the left bar.
He picked up the damaged arm when he was hit by three drunk Indians in a pick up coming the wrong way up an on ramp.
He rode well and didn't hang about.
They had a workshop in a mews on Lennox, near the lake in Oakland. It was called The Lennox Lounge and the Lizards would gather there of an evening, sat on the car seats by the big old reefer, (slang for refrigerator) drinking Miller and spinning yarns of motorcycle daring and comedy.

So consequently, because of my absence from the scene, during this period, I've no personal experience of any of the action at Brighton,

Clacton and elsewhere in '64 or over the subsequent years. Apart from working at the time, in the same place as a Mod who was one of the few captured at Clacton and did 3 months in a joint where you could be made to do bunny hops everywhere.
He was a hard looking mush but philosophical with it.

Maybe the fighting only happened at the seaside, I didn't take a lot of notice, I was having too much fun. I had a Willys Jeep, then an XK120, then a 100E van.
Yet I can't help thinking that if I'd pulled into Brighton, wearing a black leather jacket and saw an army of Mods swarming all over the promenade, I would not have got off the bike. More than any other period in history, it would have been definitely, the time to have got the hell out of Dodge.

The Rocker scene was celebrated and evolved as the 60's rolled on.
The Easy Rider generation arrived.
The outlaw clubs came into being.
The violent faction of the Mods went Skinhead.
The essential Mod vibe was preserved in Ska and Northern Soul.

As luck would have it, here we are many moons later all pals with anyone on two wheels.
All the scooters down at Brighton parked up early, to get pole position outside Volkes bar, on Rockers day.
They look ok in their Fred Perrys and little turn-ups and they are digging it.
Back in the day, the Mod fashions were generated in Soho clubs, like the Scene and the Flamingo in Wardour Street.
The style changed slightly, weekly, if not daily and the dances evolved constantly, changed by a hand move or a look.

This intense style spread in a groove, to all the pockets of Mod life in and around London.
They liked Bluebeat, Blues, Motown and old school Rhythm and Blues.
Same as a Rocker; you really have to be slim to carry it off, nowadays.
Even so, a couple of years ago watching from a Brighton pub patio, a middle aged guy kick a Lambretta, with the side panel off unsuccessfully, my girlfriend said:

Why don't you help him?

I can't. I said. Somebody might see me.
Anyway there were loads of old Mods about that would have helped him.

My mate, Harry Lyons 73, who I ride with now in the fast crowd of the South Hants Vintage Motorcycle Club, (I should really be in the intermediate crowd but there isn't one and the slow crowd is too slow), says:

If I get stopped I'm going to tell them it's the 1956 Re-enactment Society.

He has a brace of Norbsa cafe racers, amongst other things and still rides like a younger man.
He pulled into Loomies, a busy modern day, bike café near here, at the crossroads of the A32 and the A272, one day when there was a massive international scooter meet going on and announced:

I'm looking for someone who beat me up in 1964!

Amusement, laughter and banter followed. All in the best possible taste.

Ay?

HISTORICAL SNIPPETS

The term Cafe Racer didn't exist during the early sixties. A bike would be described by any racing mods that had been done to it, like clip-ons and rear-sets or an ally tank, rims, a racing seat.
A young bloke with a bike would be referred to by the general public as a Motorbike Boy.
Anyone that rode a stock bike properly was called an Enthusiast.
Bungies were called Aero-elastics.
Nobody ever used the term 'Ton-up'. Only the newspapers and people that got their information from the newspapers.
'The Ton', from the old London slang for a hundred; as in 'A Pony' for 25 and 'A Monkey' for 500, was a bit overused and round my way it was usually referred to as 'The Hundred.'
In these early days studs were not in evidence on leather jackets at least not in London. You occasionally saw a country boy with a studded jacket. You saw one or two jackets with a painted eagle or a tiger and often with the make or model of the bike.

Before the scooter became popular there was a campaign by the press and an outraged public, one summer, to stop the youth tear-arsing about on motorbikes.
I remember the front page of The Daily Mirror with a full page picture of an Ajay 31CSR. It was stood up for the photo but looked like it had hit something flat and solid at about a 100 mph.
The front end was all squeezed up behind a vertical line level with the crumpled headstock.
It made no difference; you could still buy a 650 at 16, tie on your L plates and scorch off down the by-pass.
Everybody crashed, on whatever bike they started on, some got killed.

Pete Barnbrook died the day before his 17th birthday and his folks had bought him a crash helmet for his birthday.
He was a real lad. I was a year younger than him and learned how to pull birds in the cinema from watching his technique.
The Pictures on a Sunday afternoon was a cultural event for the young people in those days. Everyone was there.
I saw him sit next to a girl, right in front of me, say a few words, put his arm round her, say a few more words and then they started snogging.
I thought. Right, that's how you do it. Tried it myself a bit more politely, of course and never looked back.
I don't do anything like that in the cinema these days, I must add. Well not since all that trouble with the vicar's wife. Only joking.

Most kids started on older smaller bikes. My 350 Beeza was rigid with teles. Well out of style. I fitted ally mudguards, sawed a couple of inches off each side of the bars and turned them upside down. I wanted the bike to sound better so I drilled a bunch of holes in the underside of the silencer.
This caught the attention of a motorbike cop as I left the cinema by Putney Bridge, my girlfriend Gin on the back, tore off up Putney High Street and up Putney Hill, without looking behind once to see him following and flew round Tibbets Corner roundabout, as only a 16 year old can, with everything scraping, in a shower of sparks.

He pulled me over. Not an uncommon experience for a young motorcyclist.

How fast did you go round that roundabout?

Ooooww, about 25.

Twenty five! He said. It was more like 45!
John Surtees couldn't have got round there any faster!

I gave it my best 'I'm not a menace to society' look. Thinking: Hmmm…. pretty fast.

At least he had a sense of humour.
He nicked me for excessive noise, because he had a new born baby at home and a loud bike kept going past his house at night and waking the baby but after close inspection still couldn't see the reason for the racket.
I didn't explain. I said I'd just bought the bike.
I was fined Ten shillings.

My biggest motorcycle disappointment was on my plunger ZB34 Gold Star; I'd bought it from Fred Launchbury's shop in Raynes Park for £32. 10.
It had clip-ons and rear sets and a TT carb.
During the time it took to accumulate the money to tax and insure it, I rode it up and down the alley at the back of my folks place. I assumed that as the gear lever was reversed then so would be the shift pattern.
First gear appeared to be so tall and, for ages, I'd been listening to folk tales and fairy stories of starship speeds reached, in first, by legendary Gold Stars and had it in my mind that this bike was going to be pretty close to being up there with the fastest.

I must have been in third all the way down to the Kingston by-pass, thinking to myself that it would probably do about 90 in second.
I nearly went over the handlebars when I shifted up, into what turned out to be a lower gear.

Clouds of woe descended momentarily but I adjusted to the fact that I didn't have a mount of the gods, just an old 500 Beeza and got on with the earthly quest for the Holy Grail.
To get to a hundred miles an hour.
The Magic Ton.

It was still out of reach, two pistons later.
I saw 95, loads of times but even taking the covers off the fork springs and the plunger units didn't get me any closer to The Hundred.

My girlfriend, Gin, from Virginia. Her name, not the state, she was from Colliers Wood, rode pillion.
From sneaking through the back streets on the way to the Palais, sitting side saddle on my first bike because her skirt was too tight, to many adventures and narrow scrapes on the ZB and the Tiger 100. Blasting off to race meetings and coastal runs, riding with Ronnie Pyle and Wendy.
I bumped into Ronnie, last year at Kempton, he still looks like Jack Elam, that cowboy in the old films, the one that looks like a real mean, gun-slinging hombre.
We always had a great laugh.
Now he has a '58 TR5 that reposed in A.E. Walkling's bicycle shop in Merton High Street. It was one of those old style bicycle shops that made their own frames.
He'd been after it for donkey's ages.
A few people knew it was there but no one could buy it.
He got it in the end and he is a worthy owner.
It shines like a burnished jewel. Stock with a few small cycle parts in chrome.

That block, on Merton High Street where the bicycle shop was that harboured his Trophy, was the block the Wimbledon Palais was on, it also had three motorbike shops: One was Russell Bros. No relation to Russell Motors.

It was Fred Russell's place; he'd been there since the days of the belt drive and the wooden piston.

He had adverts for tyres in the window that had long been out of production and he worked, in old money with a set of sockets he'd made as an apprentice.

He always had the filter tip remains of a cigarette in his mouth and a dew drop on the end of his nose, until his demise in 1982.

He was a great engineer and some of the chaps looked after him towards the end, buying a new telly, patching his roof and stuff.

Then there was Go-Well Motors, who were Gordon and Tony Bartlet, well known in trials circles. They did apprenticeships at AMC, in Plumstead. Gordon had ridden a G45 to Portsmouth on megaphones and trade plates, to run it in for a race the next day. Sitting on a wooden stool in the ivy covered and decorated, corrugated shed that extended from the back of the shop, Gordon would tap out the dents in a petrol tank through a hole cut in the bottom and weld it up beautifully.

They could do it all here. It was an old school, motorcycle workshop.

There was often one of their mates in there, telling stories and having a laugh. They later, did work for Verralls, making some of the restored bikes into working motorcycles. Some rare and exotic machines found their way through Go-Well's hallowed portals.

Abbey Spares was the other shop. It was a breakers. The entire place, upstairs and downstairs, and the yard was chocker; mountains of gearboxes, forests of fork legs, pipes, silencers, tanks, frames and everything else hanging off the ceilings and bursting at the seams.

Out front of the shop on the wide pavement stood two rows of old bikes, permanently. Nothing exiting, just old, dusty things with girder forks and cobwebs. More dust, bus tickets and toffee papers gathered by their worn out tyres.
I got to Abbey Spares a bit too late, by the time I opened Merton Motorcycle Spares in 1977, all the good stuff had gone.
The place was abandoned with both doors open.
I did take a box full of medieval rectifiers and another of unrecognizable brake plates.
I got a few bits to take up space on the shelves of my shop, which was handy because I didn't have that much stuff when I first started. Funnily enough, I did find an old Harley speedo that was meant to come my way.
Ace Motorcycles took over the shop next door and sold bikes with Len Diggins at the helm. Not Cliff Rushworth's Ace Classics but the firm that also had a shop on Brixton Hill.
There were bike shops all over the place in the early days and later on, that manor had its share of classic motorcycle establishments. Ned Smyll, of Newton and Smyll and The Bike Barn, had his first shop in Merton High Street, in the '80s. Jim Wine had a shop in Haydons Road in the '70s. Bob Harris had another, later, in the same road, which, coincidentally, is one of the roads ridden down in the film The Leather Boys.

Ronnie had a '60 Matchless G12CSR Sportstwin, the year with the kicked up silencer, he'd changed the paint to ivory, which looked great and he kept it very clean. I was always chasing after him on my plunger Gold Star. One time coming round a corner, on the A29 at Pulborough, I found a copper on point duty, directing traffic and not enough time to stop.
There was a Consul and a Lambretta stationary, waiting for directions and a keep left sign.

Braking and skidding I went between the scooter and the keep left sign, just catching the keep left sign with my footrest and crashing right in the middle of the junction at the very feet of the constable on point duty.
I looked up at him.
He still had his hands in the air, in traffic directing mode.
I stood up.
The bike lay there, oil and petrol just starting to leak.
Gin sat there, next to the bike, a tear just starting in the corner of her eye.
I picked her up first.
We were taken into the cottage right in front of the scene of the misdemeanour.
They'd had experience of this sort of thing before having had a car in their front garden more than once. The old couple gave us tea and were very nice.
I tried to slide away from the situation, unnoticed but the copper was waiting and collared me. I ended up getting done for driving without due care and attention.
The fine was a fiver with three quid costs and a month's ban. I think they went easy on me as they'd brought witnesses from as far away as Wales and had a blackboard there with a map of the junction and the vehicle positions, all for no reason as I'd pleaded guilty, already, by post.
Gin got back on the bike and we all carried on with the ride to Littlehampton, where we all had egg and chips and a laugh, by the sea.
I swapped the ZB and £20 for a '55 Tiger 100.
I had it sprayed red, fitted the later badges, got the oil tank, toolbox and rear springs chromed and changed the bars to cowhorns.
I revved the nuts off it in all the gears, tried everything I knew, which was limited, including changing the engine sprocket size up

and down in attempts to get to the hundred. It would do 95 in third and 97 in top. I eventually wore the old engine out and had to rebuild it.

I had just started hanging out at the Caprice, I knew a couple of the guys there, anyway, from school or from back before anyone had bikes.
Everyone there had plenty of chat and was up for a laugh.
There were loads of stories, tales of bravado, tales of sexual encounters, plenty of ducking and diving and bobbing and weaving and a juke box punching out tunes.
I loved Chuck Berry's Jaguar and the Thunderbird and the way he sang about Cadillacs and V8 Fords. There wasn't a good motorcycle song. So I wrote this little number:

This would have a driving down and dirty, Rock n Roll bass line, a raw guitar and be done by someone like the Steve Gibbons Band, in a basement dive, on the Isle of Man.

It goes like this:

Well I sold my motorsickle it was the fastest machine in town

I lost my licence and things are sure looking down

There's only nine of us left, out of number sixteen

My best friends died, hanging over their machines

With their motors burning R and their pipes. . . . . .pouting screams.

When I rolled back the grip I left a quarter mile o' rubber on the ground.

From ten miles off you could hear my megaphones sound.

Everyone on the road used to eat my dust

It was a methane burning missile

That satisfied my lust

With the carbs in tune, one forty.................... was a must.

Well I rode my iron with the rev counter needle on the ten.

It was a red steel stallion that separated the boys from the men.

It had twin GPs burning alcohol fuel

It was a chrome plated weapon in the highway duel

I got the century in second

On the way............................. to Sunday school.

I wrote that in 1961 when I was 17.
No excuses.
If any mega-group would care to record it I'm sure we can come to a mutually agreeable arrangement over the royalties

On the road to Southend

BOGNOR REGIS

A bunch of us first went camping in Bognor in 1959 when we were 15; we got a lift down there in Rob Gauntlet's Dad's beetle-backed Vanguard. Each year after that, we made it there at Easter or Whitson.
The popularity of this jolly boys outing grew year by year, eventually involving all the hounds we knew from the Palais and the mob from the Caprice.
One time a whole load of us pulled into a field entrance, there were bikes and cars. We parked up and clambered into a big open fronted barn.
Being from the city, nobody had an inkling that there might be country folk living in cottages, somewhere out in the darkness, with access to a phone.
Consequently a big bundle started in the barn with plenty of hollering, shouting and people chucking bales of hay at one another and blokes getting thrown off the top of hay stacks.
Inevitably the law turned up in a van.
The barn became instantly, quiet and still.
Two helmeted, dark shapes, with torches, were silhouetted against the van's lights.

Right! If you lot don't all come out now we're going to send the dogs in.

It was like a whole layer of the hay lifted as everyone rose from underneath their hastily arranged camouflage and stood with it tumbling from their heads and shoulders.

Hold up. I said to Diz. Stay here.

Our bikes were out of sight, leaning on the back of the barn, neither of them having stands. It was the middle of the night, we'd been raving it up for hours and I didn't fancy mooching about in the dark looking for somewhere else to kip.

The coppers were cool as you like, after the usual pleas of innocence and a bit of friendly banter; the Sergeant said:

I know you boys haven't come all this way, to cause any trouble. If you turn left out of here, then right, there's a barn down that lane that you can sleep in. You won't disturb anybody there.

I think it was Trout's voice I heard say:

Can we have your name in case they ask who sent us.

Gertcha. He said. Be on your way; and quietly.

That must have been the last time anything like that happened. Today a SWAT team would be sliding down ropes out of a helicopter and shooting up all of Tombstone.
It would have been '62. By 1963 things were tightening up. Youth was featuring more and more in the media and I guess the whip has to be cracked now and again but, looking back maybe that was the beginning of the end of the common sense. Dunkirk spirit. The fact that we're all in it together. Do what you like as long as you don't frighten the horses attitude that was inherited from all those who went through World War Two.
No, it's still alive in the hearts of Bikers, Hot Rodders, Psychobillys, Punks, Teddy Boys, ordinary geezers.
Everyone that understands the true meaning of Rock n Roll.

Long may it reign and spread throughout the world.

I was in another barn, another time, just off the main drag from Bognor to Littlehampton with a bunch of bikers from the Caprice, when right in the middle of the hay bale bundle that was in full swing, somebody said, loudly:

Hold up!

It all went pretty quiet.

There's someone in here!

It went deathly quiet.

Fear struck every one of us, deep in the depths of our very souls. I'm sure.

What could it be?

Could it be a monster?

A poor old tramp, all covered in hay, got up out of the corner of the barn, clutching all his worldly possessions, stepped and grunted, unevenly, through the bodies and climbed down the bales.

He must have been terrified when we turned up.

Sorry mate. Someone said.

You don't have to go.

Stay here.

He wandered off, swearing like a trooper, cursing into the night.

Whenever I stayed in a barn after that, I always introduced myself in case there was somebody else in there, already.

Another time I was looking for a place to kip, the night before the Ramsgate sprint. Grayham Carlton and I had met two girls on the prom, on the Saturday evening and had taken them for a ride which, unfortunately, as it happened, led to nothing exciting.
After dropping them off we had ridden out of Ramsgate and pulled off the road, up a dirt track into an orchard.
I had my bike on the centre stand and by the light of its headlamp was poking my way into a spot I'd found behind some bushes, under the eaves of a brick, transformer shed, when a voice from two, side by side faces all old, wrinkled and wrapped in rags, said:

GRRRRRRRRRRRRRR! FUCK OFF OUT OF IT!

I jumped back about 6 feet.
It was an old tramp couple. All cuddled up together.
I bet they were just as scared as I was with bikes turning up in the middle of nowhere.

Sorry mate. I said.

Grrrrrrr. He said.

We rode off and found somewhere else, less crowded.

Ramsgate sprint was run along the prom, which was made of concrete sections with bits of grass growing up in the joints and it was curved.
It was a damp, windswept day in autumn, the time we were there. The waves were breaking over the sea wall and splashing across the track.
Yet the sprint was held.
Old Duggies, blown Triumphs and a Vincent sidecar outfit, amongst the stuff blasting up the strip regardless.
Quite a contrast to some current drag race officials who'd knock back a flathead Ford, in a nostalgic race, over a spoonful of water from the radiator overflow.
Jobsworths.

That's enough moaning.

Well these have been a few tales from those early days; say spring 1960 to autumn 1963 and the photos to match.

Out of the boys I knew there were some who bent the rules and some who were outside the law on occasion but none of them were villains. At least one of them would have captured a machine gun nest if he'd been born 20 years earlier.

There were loads of guys doing this and always will be.

Rock and Roll is here to stay.

Johnny Willers and Keith May on the Vincent Norton. Picture taken across from the Caprice, he'd be 17 in this picture.
It was reckoned to be Lightning spec and it had enough grunt to break a back sprocket.
He built this in his backyard shed where he had a good selection of well-used engineering equipment. He'd done a bit of grass track racing and this was his first road bike.

The first time anyone ever stopped at the Mote Cafe on the A29.

The usual suspects are: Tony Latham Gold Star, Johnny Willers Vincent/Norton, Kieth May, Arfa Bevan Bonny, myself and Bonny with clip-ons and bent frame.
You can see the rake is pushed back.
It was one of the first 30 duplex framed bikes; they were built without the lower top tube to the frame. I was told this by one of the mechanics at Hughes, the pure Triumph spares and repairs only, shop on the Colliers Wood/Tooting bridge.
A slow contact with the front bumper of a car, whilst riding with one hand off the bars, talking over my shoulder, to a mate on the

pillion, round the back of some lock-ups, bent the headstock back a good few degrees.
The only other damage being to my orchestras.

Triumphs did a re-call. You could swap the front part of the frame but this one still had its original factory set up.
Both down tubes eventually cracked right through.
A mate of Bugsy's at Durnsford Road power station welded a dirty-great lump of iron across everything under the headstock.
It held the frame together but caused the bike to vibrate severely with the subsequent loss of power.
This was resolved one day when I was racing Diz on his Hundred and Ten down a long residential road.
We were side by side, at about a hundred and he was pulling away.
A terrible humiliation for a Bonneville owner.
Luckily, the weld snapped on the frame repair, the motor hung down in a more comfortable position, the vibration stopped and the bike surged forward into the lead.
I had to use both sides of the road to get round the bend under a railway bridge because the bike didn't want to go where I aimed it but I did get to the Caprice before him.
I got hold of another frame which made my motorcycling much more enjoyable.

The '59 T.110 is Aussie's and that's Martin Small with his Dommi. Aussie took this picture. He was always the last to arrive anywhere. His excuse was that he had no nuts on his top shock absorber bolts. I don't think he ever did get any nuts on his top shock absorber bolts.

No Mods about in 62

This snap was taken in an ordinary cafe, in a side road in Littlehampton.
Some of the chaps from the Caprice enjoy a spot of supper before a night in a barn.
Arthur Bevan, Aussie, me, Colin (Harry) Monk, Mick Ellington, Big Mac, John Emans, Arthur Winner, Keith May, John Willers, Malcolm, Bob, Dizzy Evans, Tony Latham, Tony George with the pie and beans and in the foreground the Eaton Clubman chukka boot of Johnny Sullivan.

I don't remember anything untoward occurring in the café, probably just the usual laughing and joking and recounting events of the ride

there, piss-takes of people's bloomers and near misses accompanied by bouts of laughter.
The harmless shenanigans of youth but someone must have mentioned our presence to the police, because as we were nearly ready for the off, manoeuvring the bikes outside in the road, a big old sergeant, flanked by two constables came walking down the centre of the narrow little road, like in gunfight at the OK corral.

It's the coppers! Someone shouted over the racket kicked up by 10 bikes starting up and echoing back off all the buildings.

Some turned and went back the wrong way down the one-way street.
Some rode past the coppers on the pavement.
When the cops lunged for one guy, another shot past them, they dived for him and the first guy they went for escaped.
All in a dark side street, mainly lit by slashing headlight beams with a soundtrack of roaring engines and hollers and shouts of:

Come back 'ere you little fuckers!

We re-grouped at a darkened corner on the outskirts of town then went in search of a barn for the night's kip.

Them crazy fools will race anywhere.

Tony and me outside Comerfords, on a little Saturday afternoon jaunt. You could blast down the Kingston by-pass then cut through the lanes down to Thames Ditton to check out the hundreds of new and used bikes they had there.
They got cheaper, the deeper you went into the shop, until you got right to the back, where all the old nails were, more or less, leaning on each other.
This was the row my first bike came from.
Yet, when the kickstart spring broke they fixed it, free of charge.
A good after sales service on a mere £26 bike.

Speed cop looks, incredulously, at John's NorVin. The bike was up together, he was never nicked for anything mechanical, mostly the cops just wanted to have a look at it.
This shot was taken by the lay-by on the Mickleham by-pass, the bit of the A24 that runs along the bottom of Box Hill.

By his 60 Bonnie is Vic Willoughby, killed just days after this Sunday.

You either hung out up by the cafe at the top of Box Hill or here, the lay-by on the Mickleham by-pass, to watch the bikes go by, generally flat out.
Not every Sunday but sometimes there would be speed cops, poodling about on Speedtwins or Thunderbirds.
No contest there then.
I have a memory of a Gold Star going by at speed with a police Wolesley 110 in hot pursuit, bells ringing.
The girl on the pillion was looking back and doing V signs as the rider wove in and out of the Sunday traffic.
A big cheer went up from the lay-by.

Graham Carlton on the Shooting Star he bought new, on which he immediately fitted Gold Star clip-ons, headlight brackets and rear sets.
Myself and Tony George in the background.
Can't recognize the speed merchant in the far carriageway

A man without a stand on his bike can instinctively spot a handy parking place.

John had that helmet built up on the sides with a peak moulded in. It looked like a Korean War, pilot's helmet. He built this Vincent Norton in a shed that took up most of the backyard of the little terraced house in Mitcham and scorched it about the streets dealing, with all its idiosyncrasies. He sorted the handling after an instant whip practice day at Brands, ran it at the Brighton Speed Trials and at various tracks. It eventually evolved into a polished, engineering masterpiece.

Martin's 600 Dommi with DMD dustbin. Well most of it.

Photo opportunity for Vic, Arthur, Malcom, John, Jerry Clayton, Diz and Graham Carlton.

The long gone lay-by on the Mickleham by-pass, the bit of the A24 that runs along the bottom of Box Hill. On a Sunday afternoon it was a place to call in to if you just fancied a little blat out into the countryside.

A couple of the first blurry colour photos taken, outside the Caprice, by Ginger McRae, who is responsible for most of these pics.

The Caprice was just a local cafe. Occasionally a passing biker would stop and chat. People would come and go or join in and never leave. There was little aggravation and only the occasional grudge drag from outside the cafe to the end of the road, about an 1/8th of a mile, late at night, ever so slightly disturbing the peace when everything else was shut.

Inane biker activity featuring Dick the Caveman, Pete, Bimbo, Alex, me, Big Mac, Diz and Janet.
Big Mac was in the motorcycle business and later, raced a Manx and Hughsey's Triumph on the Island.

Snow in the air. The long winter of 62/63. I'd polished the rockers, shortened and tapered the valve guides, polished the ports and was looking forward to better weather. It snowed until April. I did try and get the hundred in the snow on the Kingston by-pass, one Sunday but even with encouragement from a bunch of nutters waving me on from the back window of a Mk 2 Jag I couldn't get more than 95 with my goggles up or down. I had him away from the Toby Jug lights but my gear lever fell off. The Jag went flying past. They looked as disappointed as me that we weren't racing. I waved goodbye as I pulled over then walked back and found it in the piled up snow at the edge of the fast lane.

Cameras were rare in those days and a photo occasion was always interesting enough to get a bunch of poseurs outside in the middle of winter.

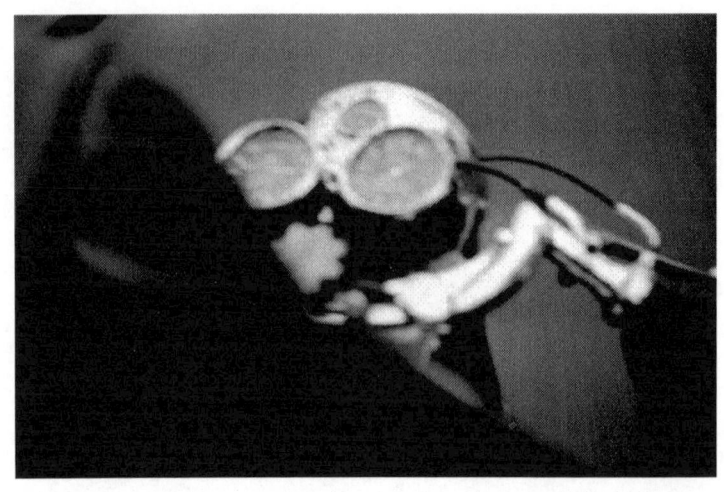

Down the coast. Bill Brown AJS 31 CSR with DMD fairing, Pete (Septimus) Dean Velo, Rob Smith Super Rocket. 1961

Rob Smith, in designer wellies and Pauline, with his 650SS outside the Caprice.

Rob's dad filled those wellies with water, one time, in an effort to persuade his son to buy himself some better foot wear. Rob rode to Brighton in his slippers whilst his wellies were drying.

Turned down wellingtons were the choice of many young bikers starting out. Most worked their way up to proper boots. Yet some have stayed loyal to the well worn rubber boot over the years. Don Blake whom I met on VMCC runs, down here in the South, still wears 'em riding his well used Garden Gate Manx. He is in his 80s and those old wellies have been to the Elephant and the Dragon rallies, even recently.

Drop the clutch ! I'm not pushing it all the way.

Tony George capering for the camera.

Gworn my son!

A few of us were about a mile into an evening run to Box Hill when Tony with Layna as passenger flew into a roundabout, got half way round then slid off in a tarmac gauging shower of sparks and gravel. We all stopped.
He picked the bike up, looked it over and asked Layna if she was ok.

Yeah. She said dusting herself down and rearranging her hair.

He rocked the Constellation off the stand and kicked it into life.

Don't go so mad. She said as she slung her leg over the pillion.

Ok. Said Tony.

Vic, Robert (Bomber) Newton, Malcom, Johnny Willers, Colin (Harry) Monk, John Emans, Ray (Winkle) Stocker and Graham (Bugsy) Burnett.

Bimbo bought his SS Dominator and gradually de-tuned it, selling the rev counter and the twin carbs. It was said that he rode so slow that he got nicked for parking one time, while he was riding home.

Tony George on Ginger McRae's 61 bought from Guivers in Sutton in 1962. The guy in Guivers was named Vern which, coincidentally, was the name of the guy in Hughes the local, pure Triumph only spares dealer. We were spoiled for Triumph dealers at that time. Elite Motors was only up the road, in Tooting and they carried spares for all the major marques.
I had to go up to Vauxhall, to Harveys to get a '60 Bonnie oil tank one Saturday morning. It was only a small shop but they had loads of everything Triumph.
They had a couple or three guys serving, just selling spares and the queue was out the door and along the road.
I was in a hurry to get an oil tank and never did cure the cracking brackets in spite of severe rubber mounting. Just always had an oil

tank being welded at any one time so I could quickly swap it over and get back in the race.

The engine would willingly rev to 8500 but could vibrate your feet off the footrests if you didn't have a grip.

Just to show what can be done, a well balanced 650 Triumph was clocked at 143 mph at the Highlander in practise for the '69 TT production race, in which, it lapped at over 100 mph.

Vern in Hughes, he was referred to as Hughesy, was offended, outraged and irritated by young herberts cutting bits off their bikes, fitting high bars or clip-ons and especially when later model badges or parts were fitted to an earlier machine.

His eyes would go to the ceiling in despair when you asked for a bit for your bike that was never ever fitted by the factory.

It was a great shop. Ned Smyll took it over, decades later and I got to look round.

It was on 4 floors, dropping down from the bridge, to the side of the railway line, out back. Ned had it chocker with British stuff, in the old school tradition.

HAYLING ISLAND

Johnny Sullivan, '56 T110, me, '60 T120 and Bomber Newton, '58 Road Rocket on the way to breakfast after a night kipping on the beach.

Aussie Austin, Johnny Sullivan, Bugsy, Diz, Sep (after Septimus the Spider, in the Dandy) and Ray Stocker pose it up, after breakfast.

Another jolly boys outing, to Hayling Island. This picture taken on Southsea seafront.

Roaring through quiet, night time villages on the way there. Loads of harmless lunacy, entertaining ourselves, down by the sea, a few hours' uncomfortable kip and more of the same the next day.

This was Whitsun '62, beside the little Big Dipper at Littlehampton.

They just showed themselves.

Oh I do like to be beside the seaside.

Beside the seaside

Beside the sea.

Mole Russell went to John o'Groats on this Shooting Star.
Martin went on to give his Dommi the full cafe racer treatment.
Ridden winter and summer, Bomber's Road Rocket aquired the
well used look.

Triumph fans showing their appreciation of a BSA

Do something nice for the photo Bomber

They don't make 'em like that anymore.

The things you find in farmer's fields.

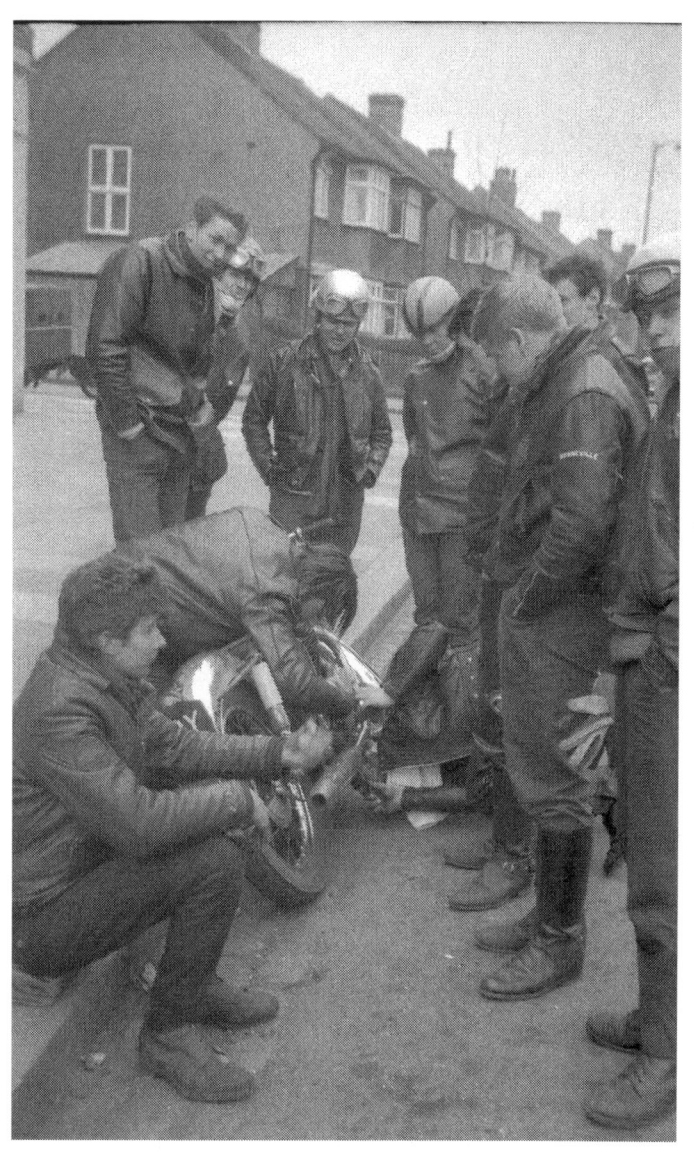

A bit of routine maintenance.

Mavis at the controls, Dick the Caveman chuckling.

Dick the Caveman, so called because he had long hair before anyone did and walked like a caveman because of much broken limb, scrambling damage.
He married Maggie and their first child was born in his lock-up garage.
To get there you went through a horse and cart sized brick arch in a row of terraced Victorian workers houses.

It was between Bernies Caff and The Prince of Wales, opposite the Morden factory estate and it opened out into a circle of lock-ups, between the railway line and a rugby pitch, almost like a holiday village or a motel on a backroad in Boondock county.

There was a grassy area, in the middle, where reclined a trio of V8 Pilots.

Dick's lock-up had central heating and it was also home to a V twin J.A.P sprinter called Bloody Mary.

The snooker hall doorway on the left and the bogs on the right . . .

What are we waiting for?

Bolt that bit back on and we can go . . .

Tony, me and Aussie pose it up in the alley.

John Emans with his TR5

Les girls: Cathy Hutchins and Brenda.

Oberleutenant Martin Small, the smiling storm trooper.

Girls just wanna have fun.

Don't try this at home

How many monkeys can you get on a motorbike?

Gin and me with my 1951 ZB34 Gold Star at 17 in 1961. I bought the DBD tank for £1 from Dave Bond who lived near me. He had replaced it with a new 5 gallon ally tank on his new Goldie. The day I went to his place to pick it up he had the detonated remains of his engine littered about the floor of his garden shed. A snapped con rod, smashed cases, bits of piston and liner here and there amongst the devastation. I felt bad just looking at it. I dread to imagine how he must have felt. The bike was only a month old.
He'd been trying to do 80 in first.

The ZB wasn't the one to have at the time, not being the swinging arm model but it was still exciting to ride, what with its poor handling and inadequate brakes.
I melted 2 pistons trying to get to the Ton but only ever got to see 95.

Little Mac who was in fact tall but not as big as Big Mac.

Ginger McRae and Vic Willoughby. Bonnevilles are us

Jolly boys outing to Margate.

Doctor Who?

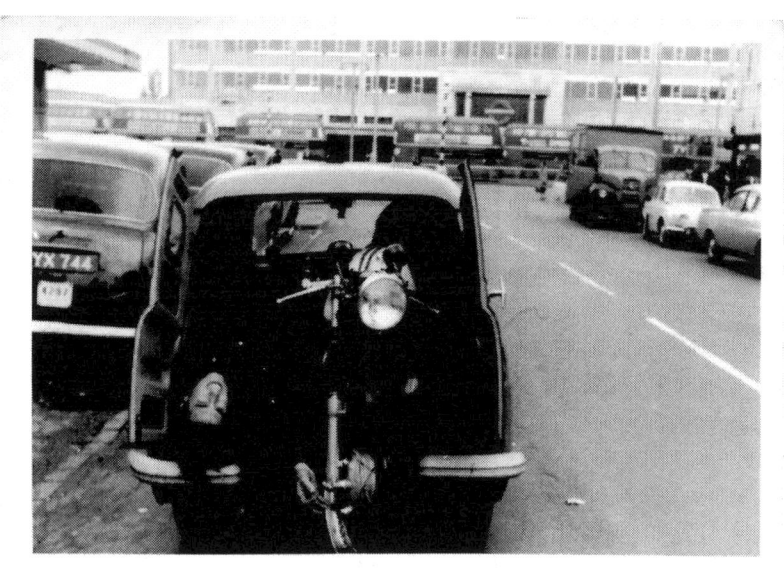

Rob Smith dramatizing an otherwise uneventful bike pick up.

Skylarking about in the Caprice – Always something going on.

In borrowed titfers, Dino and Frank do 'Regrets, I've had a few'

Trying Ernie Parish's bike for comfort. Later on he passed me at about 80 on the frozen snow at the side of the Kingston by-pass. This 60 Bonneville now resides in Ace Classics. Restored with new old stock tanks and cycle parts.

Outside the pub

Inside the cafe

I've got the culprits right here.

Say... Testicles!

Diz at Duxford

The bike he christened Loki, started out as a 50 quid Tiger 110 from Pride and Clarks. He eventually built a frame for it and ran a slick. I can't remember any times but I did have a go on it once and it took off like a scalded Tiger 110.

Ginger launches

Ginger McRae bought this 61 Bonneville brand new in 1962 from Guivers in Sutton. It was a small bike shop that did repairs and a general selection of spares. They didn't sell new bikes but they had this one and it stood there in the window for a year. He gave £250 for it which was a good deal as the price of a new 62 was creeping up towards £300.

Ginger was the guy that had the camera and is responsible for most of these pics. He is the historian for this little cultural and social episode in a far flung corner of the motorcycle world and he still is the one to let all the old pals know when the next curry night is occurring.

John lays rubber.

This shot is reminiscent of the picture of this bike on the cover of Motorcycle Mechanics. Johnny Willers built this bike in his shed. It evolved to be center stage on the Solvol Autosol stand at Earls Court. Polished to the hilt. He took it with him when he went to America, decades ago. I think it's in Japan currently.

The pits at Duxford

This is the bike I'd seen outside Johnsons when it had a road race tank and number plates.

I reckon that this had to be the bike I envisioned when I wrote that song, a couple of years before…

A red steel Stallion . . .

Twin GPs burning alcohol fuel . . .

A chrome plated weapon in the highway duel . . .

And polished alloy, even better . .

A masterpiece.

This snap was taken at the sprint at Duxford; when I saw it at Johnsons, on its ally road tank, was painted the letters JL and a little row of bombs like on a warplane.
I took it to mean the number of burn ups he'd won against significant people.
The word was that a bloke turned up one day, at Johnsons with a full monty racing Vincent, in a van and had him out on the road.

The Sutton by-pass, in the afternoon.

The Sutton By-Pass was the local drag strip. If all the story telling, all the put downs of particular bikes and the claims of top speeds had to be seen to be proven then it would be a race from the lights to the bridge, heading back towards Rose Hill, reckoned to be a quarter mile and the absolute test of who had the fastest bike.

In the pits by the lights.

The idea is to go through, turn around, line up at the lights and take off in this direction.

Lights to the bridge. The local ¼ mile.

650SS Norton versus 700 Royal Enfield Constellation.

The Sutton by-pass was not as exciting as the Kingston but it was only a mile from the Caprice and was handy for road tests and grudge races.

One sunny Saturday afternoon a bunch of us were reclining on the grass, up by the Rosehill roundabout with the bikes parked in the cycle lane when the cops pulled up and walked over to us.

Have you lot been racing up and down here ?

No, not us.

We've had reports of bikes being ridden along here at high speed.

Must have been somebody else, it wasn't us. We've only just got here.

Just then an old boy, in a flat cap and a wartime raincoat, pop-popped by, on a Bantam, about 35 mph.

There you go officer that must be one of 'em. Somebody said.

Some bloke who was going out with Big Mac's younger sister, doing a bit of routine maintenance.

Kids that thrash the nuts off their bikes are forever adjusting chains, clutches, ignitions, carburettors and constantly bolting things back on. One of the few things good about getting older is that your bike needs less maintenance.

Robert Bomber Newton on Dizzy's One One O. The paint was done by H.E.Green's bicycle shop, just along from the cafe. They could do that polychromatic stove enamel like you saw on bicycle frames and divide the colours with a coach line. There were quite a few Triumphs about with variations on the two-tone style: Red and Blue, Orange and Silver to name but a few. Bugsy had his Shooting Star in Canary Yellow.

Diz on my Tiger 100. We were mates from the age of 10. He was killed in a car wreck in 1986. We gave a fiver for this Mercury.

A couple of beers on a Friday night at the Morden Tavern.

All this without drugs.

Aussie Austin, Mole Russell and girlfriends leave the Morden Tavern on a Friday, generally the only night anyone went to the pub for beer and cockles.
It was a big old estate pub that had seen better days.
The music was from a sing-along piano accompanied by a bass drum, a snare drum and a cymbal.
Ginger, Diz and I stood up, one night and did our version of By the Light of the Silvery Moon, in the pub singer's style. We knew all the words because Little Richard had a version in the Hit Parade at the time.

Johnny Sullivan on Aussie's '59 110. The first days of ownership.
As it was for my '60 Bonnie.

Bugs and I celebrating our out-running a police Noddy bike in Forest Hill early Sunday morning on our way back from Southend. Earlier that day, after kipping in the beach huts, we were all riding along the prom looking for a cafe that was open when I heard a hint of mechanical failure and looked down the left side of the engine to see the primary chaincase breaking up into big chunks like in an earthquake. The link had come apart in the primary chain.

I removed some of the screwed down broken bits of the outer cover and found the back part of the link with the pins, slightly the worse for wear then walked back down the road to where it started to happen and found just the little, fish shaped spring clip, in the gutter. Not the plate that goes behind it. The footrest wasn't a problem because I had rear-sets at the time. I got home with just the clip holding the chain together.
Needless to say I've always carried spare links since then.
Well most of the time.

We had a swift, easy ride through Essex. A white line blast through the single carriageway Blackwall Tunnel then an easy saunter through the quiet Sunday morning streets of South East London.
About 5 bikes, crackling away.
Getting a bit of echo back off the buildings, now and again.
The sun was shining.
We were all wending our merry way at an enjoyable pace, probably over the speed limit but comfortable for a Sunday morning.
I stopped at a red light to see all the other bikes, one after the other ride straight through it.
I looked behind to see a Noddy bike coming up real slow.
The lights changed and he overtook me as I pulled away and gave the signal for me to pull over.
I would never have been able to show my face in the cafe, ever again, if I'd have been the only one nicked and by a Noddy.
Bugs hung his foot round the plate and I gave the copper an apologetic, better luck next time wave.

Another time I was belled by an unmarked, grey and blue Austin 105.
The two high- ranking, white shirted coppers inside were laughing as they pulled alongside, flicking their hands for me to pull over, in

a smug indication that I was going to be well and truly nicked for speeding. This was on a bit of dual carriageway on the other side of Croydon.
It led down to a T junction and there were two lanes of cars waiting there, to make the turn. I stalled my pulling over with a few hand signals and communicated that I intended to do so but managed to hold out from doing it until I could squirt down the inside of the cars, make a left and indeed my getaway.
Now I had 4 endorsements and had been banned once so I did not need another nicking.
I dropped off Loraine at the Caprice and Martin followed me up to Croydon where I parked the bike in a safe, office car park, took off the plug leads so no opportunist thief could ride off on it and reported the bike stolen from the fair on Mitcham Common.
All this I felt necessary because they were behind me, for so long, waiting for me to pull over; they must have got my number.
The police had recovered the bike when I called the next day, to see if had been found.

It's only missing the spark plug leads. Said the lady at Croydon nick.

That's handy. I said. I've got a spare pair of those.

I'll be over, shortly, to pick it up, cheers.

Some you win and some you lose. .

Sometimes you get the piston broke blues. . .

It's never really been a case of 'the older I get the faster I was' because I always exaggerated back in the day. . . yet the Bonnie I had back then did seem faster than any 650 Triumph I've ridden since. . .was it the good petrol, maybe the atmospherics or could it have been the rider weighing in a couple of stone lighter?
The mystery is lost in the mists of time.

You know it's a thrill to see the speedo needle go past 100 mph.

Even today The Ton is still Magic.

Printed in Great Britain
by Amazon